# TALL SHIPS
## AND THE
## CUTTY SARK
## RACES

# TALL SHIPS
## AND THE
## CUTTY SARK
## RACES
### PAUL BISHOP

AIDAN ELLIS

# ACKNOWLEDGEMENTS

This book has only been possible because of the kind support and information I have received from the organisations that operate the ships which I have included. Wherever possible, I have checked facts with primary sources.

Special thanks, however, must go to:

The Chairman of Berry Bros & Rudd and to those who work for Cutty Sark Scots Whisky in support of the races. Many of the excellent photographs are courtesy of Cutty Sark Scots Whisky;

The Chairman of the Sail Training Association's Racing Committee and his team;

Janka Bielak, who has allowed me to use many of her excellent photographs to illustrate this book. With her profound knowledge of sail training, Janka has a unique talent of being able to capture the true spirit of the Cutty Sark Races in her photographs;

John Hamilton, who has personally done more for sail training and the races than anyone else. A man who has inspired countless young trainees, captains and many other individuals who have been involved with sail training and the races;

My publisher, who has always had faith in my vision of completing this publication;

Colin and Rosemary Mudie;

and to my wife, Dawn.

Cutty Sark Scots Whisky has kindly provided some of the photographs in this book and allowed the use of their name and logo. They take no responsibility for the text or for the production of the book.

First published in the United Kingdom by Aidan Ellis Publishing, Cobb House, Nuffield, Henley on Thames, Oxon, RG9 5RT

First edition 1994

A CIP catalogue record for this book is available from the British Library

Design by Craig Dodd

Page make-up and typesetting by Contour Typesetters, Southall, Middx UB2 4BD

Text film and colour reproduction by D P Graphics, Bath

Printed in Italy by Vincenzo Bona srl, Turin

ISBN 0 85628 221 9

Half-title and title page photographs: Cutty Sark Scots Whisky

# CONTENTS

# DEDICATION

This book is dedicated to all captains who have inspired and guided the young through their arduous path to adulthood by providing them with the rich experience of life at sea. To all those captains who are at sea today continuing this demanding profession, and to all the young trainees who aspire to become a sail training captain themselves one day and who in turn will inspire future generations.

Never have I met a more generous and warm hearted man. He was kind to his crew, respected their feelings and did all in his power to promote their comfort. At the same time he preserved discipline and made every man know his place. A better sailor never walked a ship's planks. He understood his duty from beginning to end, kept within the bounds of authority, and, while faithful to the interests of the owners, gave every crew their full complement of provisions, and encouraged them in their enjoyments. The consequence was they respected him, and made themselves active and useful. Brave, energetic and liberal, he set an example that excited the emulation of all on board. No man flinched from danger, avoided work, or refused to share the best he had with his shipmates.

John Ross Browne
Etchings of a Whaling Cruise

# FOREWORD

Each year between 80 and 130 sail training vessels, carrying as many as 3,000 young trainees, take part in what are known as the Cutty Sark Tall Ships' Races. Some of the trainees are at the beginning of a career as professional seamen, most are enjoying a once-in-a-lifetime experience of life at sea in a vessel propelled by the wind. The vessels they sail range from small 40-foot long yachts to the full size square-riggers built in a bygone age and now adapted to cadet training.

Sail training is not like mountaineering, largely an individualistic sport. It is all about learning to face nature in a strange maritime environment as part of a team. This involves learning the give and take necessary to live together in crowded cabins, sharing the difficulties and dangers, and finally the satisfaction and triumph of a safe arrival at the desired destination. In every respect, the process is character developing since you cannot just give up and go to bed when things get tough at sea, the survival of the team depends upon everyone's ability to ensure that the ship lives through whatever arises. The fact that this may cause the trainee to learn to endure far longer than they thought was their capability is just another part of the learning process.

But it is not just the participants who gain from the experience. It used to be said that the greatest congregation of the British took place at the Derby. This is no longer the case if recent Tall Ships' Races are anything to go by with half a million becoming a small turnout, a million being the average. People everywhere flock to see the wonderful sight of a square-rigger effortlessly moving across the sea. It brings back nostalgia for an age gone past when such sights were common around the coasts of Britain.

As Chairman of the Sail Training Association, which organises these races and operates two of the ships, I have become closely involved with these spectacular gatherings and have indeed taken part. I hope all those who have any salt water in their blood will find this book, with its lovely photographs and mass of technical detail, an aid to a greater appreciation of what the Cutty Sark Tall Ships' Races mean and the true value of training in sail that they provide.

Robin Knox-Johnston, C.B.E.

Photograph: Cutty Sark Scots Whisky

# INTRODUCTION

It was the third line squall that night, blackness had suddenly enveloped our world and with it came the screaming wind. Already well reefed down and a small jib set, *Canada Maritime* began to resonate as her speed accelerated past the eleven knot barrier. At something approaching twenty knots, down the breaking face of a towering Atlantic sea, our maxi was thrown around into a broach sending books, tools, bedding and galley equipment cascading across the yacht. With the mast almost level and part of the onwatch crew momentarily engulfed by the sea, she began to recover and a quick head-count revealed that, thankfully, everyone was still attached by their safety harnesses.

That night, the mighty US Coastguard square-rigger was rolled so far over that the ends of her lower yards dipped into the sea with crew aloft. The new Polish full-rigged ship, *Dar Mlodziezy* blew out many of her sails and the Dutch naval yacht *Urania* was almost swamped when a breaking sea ripped off one of her hatches.

The next morning we learnt of the gravest tragedy, the *Marques* had sailed under with the loss of nineteen lives. Only nine members of her twenty-eight crew had survived. For us, in our hearts, the race was over. Our goal and motivation to become the first vessel to cross the finishing line off Halifax was gone and it was time to reflect . . .

The rest of the Tall Ships fleet arrived in Halifax, ensigns lowered at half mast in respect. As with a family, the crews shared their sorrow with each other and began to come to terms with the sad loss, the first ever to beset a Tall Ships' Race.

In an elegant church in Halifax, the many international crews were congregating for the memorial service, but the USSR crew of the four-masted barque *Kruzenshtern* were not expected to attend as this would be against the Soviet doctrine. Then, the whispered words 'the Russians are coming' spread through the crowds, and the captains and crews turned to see the arrival of a hundred of *Kruzenshtern's* uniformed cadets. Another step in international understanding had taken place, the captain had defied his KGB officer to bring his crew to the very moving memorial service. He had risked his career and privileges for what he believed to be right, the international 'family' was united. The sea had been our bridge.

During that race we had experienced some of our best moments and some of our worst. We had all grown older and hopefully wiser, and had become more disciplined, which was to help us in future years. We had learnt how dependent we are on each other, and of our own vulnerability. We had cultivated many friendships with 'those who should be distrusted' from behind the Iron Curtain, and had grown to realise that true human values are shared worldwide – the sea has no borders.

A decade later the process of building international understanding has continued and although the Iron Curtain has fallen, the work of the Sail Training Association is as important today as it was during the height of the Cold War. How much the Sail Training Association's work has helped, and will help, is hard to quantify. After all there are only 2,500 participants each year, but such a positive message cannot be ignored, not only by those who crew these magnificent ships but by the hundreds of thousands of spectators who witness the gatherings each year.

It is my hope that this book will not only describe the beautiful ships that grace the Cutty Sark Races in technical and historical detail, but it will describe the enormous benefits that are available to the individuals who crew them and, in turn, how this helps to build international understanding.

Photograph overleaf: Janka Bielak

Photographs opposite and above: Cutty Sark Scots Whisky

# TALL SHIPS RIGS

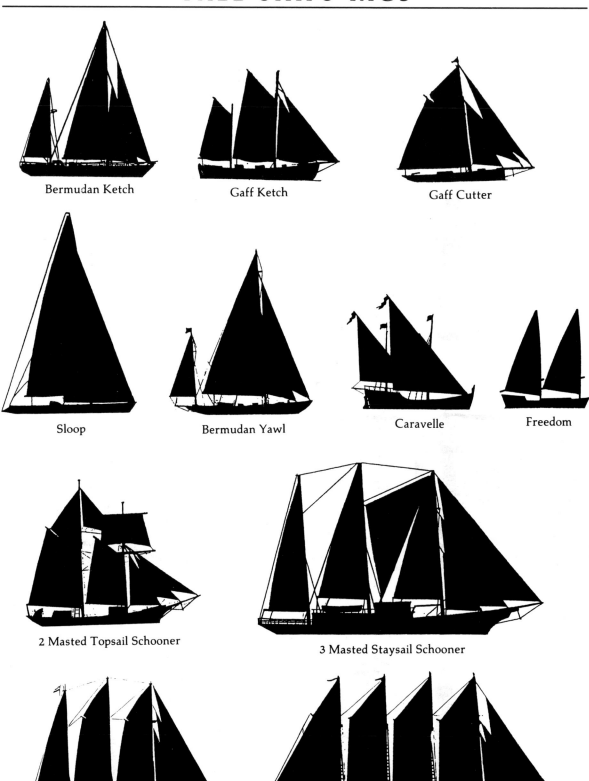

Bermudan Ketch

Gaff Ketch

Gaff Cutter

Sloop

Bermudan Yawl

Caravelle

Freedom

2 Masted Topsail Schooner

3 Masted Staysail Schooner

3 Masted Schooner

4 Masted Schooner

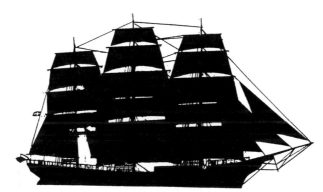

Full-rigged Ship

Brig

Brigantine

3 Masted Barque

Barquentine

4 Masted Barque

# SAIL PLANS

1 Mainsail
2 Jib
3 Staysail
4 Mizzen
5 Foresail
6 Jib Topsail
7 Topmast Staysail
8 Course
9 Lower Topsail
10 Upper Topsail
11 Topgallant
12 Royal
13 Spanker
14 Flying Jib
15 Outer Jib
16 Inner Jib
17 Fore Topmast Staysail
18 Mizzen Topsail
19 Topgallant Staysail
20 Royal Staysail

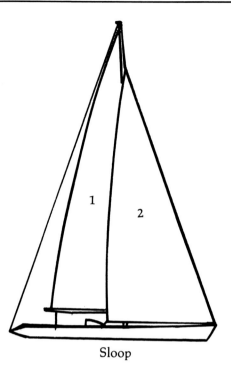

Sloop

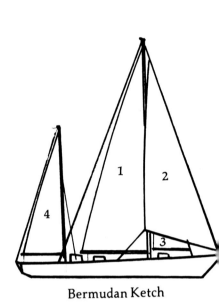

Bermudan Ketch

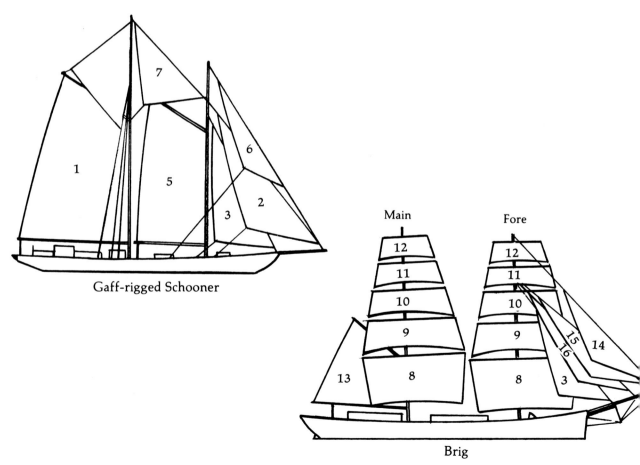

Gaff-rigged Schooner

Brig

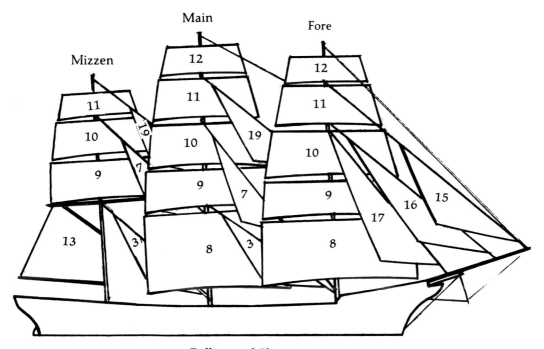

Mizzen   Main   Fore

Full-rigged Ship

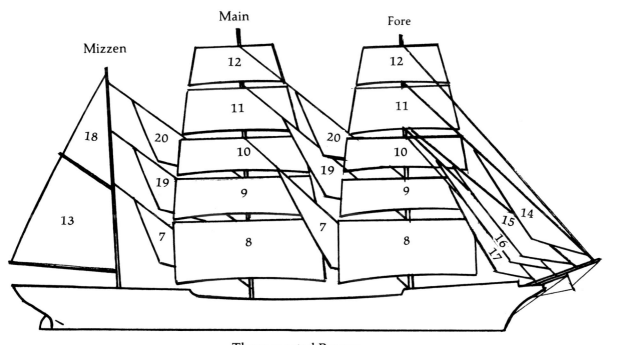

Mizzen   Main   Fore

Three-masted Barque

# SAIL REDUCTION

When the wind gets stronger the sails get smaller and fewer.

**Up to Force 5**

A barquentine with all sails set in winds below 22 knots.

**Above Force 6**

The wind has now reached about 35 knots and the crew have shortened sail. There is a reef in the mizzen and mainsail and the crew have handed 3 of the barquentines squaresails leaving only lower and upper topsail. The maintopmast and topgallant staysails and the jib and staysail remain set.

# THE MIGHTY, MAXI AND MINI

**Above Force 10**

The barquentine is now experiencing extreme conditions and has set her storm canvas. This includes her mizzen and main trysail and her storm jib, staysail and main staysail.

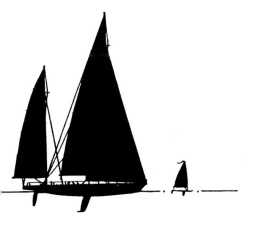

A comparison of sizes; SEDOV, the largest ship in commission today with STEINLAGER, the famous winner of the 1991 Whitbread Round the World Race, and the most numerous class of vessel in the world, a Laser dinghy.

# UNDER SAIL

During the last century the rig of a 'windjammer' had been refined for the sole purpose of harnessing the wind in order to power the vessel across the oceans and seas of the world. The complex web of rope, wires and canvas has changed surprisingly little since then and it still takes skill, discipline, courage and teamwork to manage it.

A ship sails in a dynamic environment, with the wind and sea constantly changing, and therefore the rig requires continual adjustment to ensure that she is being propelled efficiently. She needs to be balanced so that she is easy to steer and this is achieved by setting the sails correctly and 'handing sail' if the wind increases (see Sail Reduction). If a ship is not balanced properly, she will slow down as the rudder will have a braking affect, and if she is trying to claw to windward and she has too much canvas set, she will heel over excessively and be pushed sideways (leeway).

To sail a ship on a steady course at her best speed demands hard work and skill from the crew, but when she is put through one of the manoeuvres outlined below, an extra degree of concentration and teamwork is required from the crew.

## Tacking Ship

Although the rigging of a square-rigged ship is designed for the wind to be captured from astern, this manoevure entails heading into the wind and can be carried out if the wind is not too strong (or too light). The advantage of 'tacking ship' is that she will not lose any of the hard-won distance that she has made to windward.

1 The ship will not be able to sail forward in the 'no go zone' and will need to rely on her own momentum to carry her into the first stage of tacking. Therefore the ship is sailed 'free' to gain the necessary speed to execute the manoeuvre;

2 The jibs are 'let fly' as she opposes the turn;

3 The sails begin to 'lift' as she begins to come around;

4 The squaresails on the main mast are braced which helps push the stern of the ship around. The spanker can be hauled to windward which will help 'weathercock' her into the wind. She might even start sailing backwards for a while and this would mean applying reverse helm;

5 The squaresails on the foremast are still in the original braced position pushing the bow of the vessel through the wind;

6 The squaresails on the foremast are finally braced around and the headsails are taken across once the ship is out of the 'no go zone', allowing her to sail off on the other tack.

## Wearing Ship (Gybing)

This manoevure is usually carried out in heavy weather or light winds. It is a relatively simple manoeuvre for a square-rigged ship as the stern is passed through the wind, keeping the wind from astern. Complete control can be maintained as she will not lose any significant speed or steerage way. Considerable ground is lost during this evolution.

1 The spanker might be brailed to ease the turn. The helm is then put over to start the procedure;

2 The main mast squaresails are squared and stalled allowing the stern to come through the wind. The foremast squaresails are continually adjusted as the ship comes around;

3 The headsails are brought across and the ship sails off on the other tack.

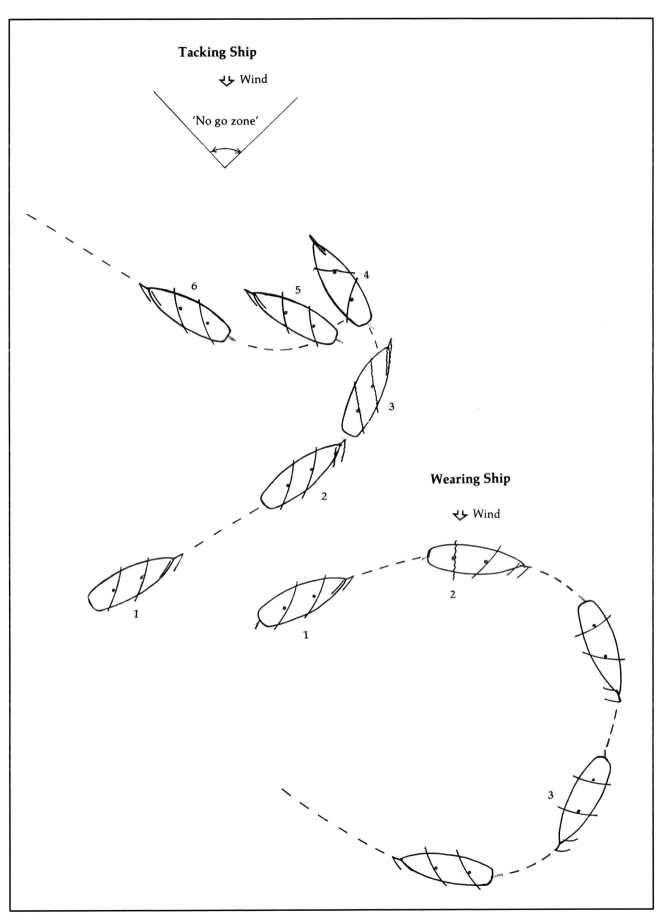

**Tacking Ship**

Wind

'No go zone'

**Wearing Ship**

Wind

## Box Hauling

Unique to square-riggers, this method of wearing ship has the benefit of not losing so much of the valuable ground that has been gained to windward. It is sometimes used in light airs if the vessel does not have the momentum to tack. This traditional evolution starts as if she were being tacked, but the squaresails on the foremast are backed, creating sternway and forcing the bow to 'pay off' with the helm reversed. The spanker might be brailed and the squaresails on the mainmast are squared. When the bow has 'payed off' sufficiently, the helm is put over and this manoeuvre continues as wearing ship.

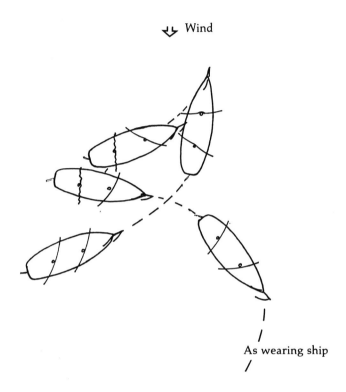

↙ Wind

As wearing ship

## Heaving-to

A handy manoeuvre for a square-rigger which is often used for man-overboard drills, taking on pilots etc.

↙ Wind

Slow drift to leeward

# THE CUTTY SARK TALL SHIPS' RACES

## A RACE TO SELF DISCOVERY AND INTERNATIONAL UNDERSTANDING

Every year over two thousand young people from many nations race together at sea under sail in the Cutty Sark Tall Ships' Races. These races are organised by the Sail Training Association and sponsored by Cutty Sark Scots Whisky. They attract a diversity of vessels from modern maxi yachts to the largest windjammers afloat today.

Staged in some of the most bustling and scenic ports in the world, the race series are broadly held in rotation in the Baltic, Biscay, North Sea, around the British Isles and across the Atlantic. The young people who crew these vessels are provided with an excellent opportunity to visit many interesting host ports, not only to celebrate their successes in the race with 'a good run ashore', but to enter the many inter-ship competitions and enjoy the entertainment laid on to encourage the building of international friendship between the myriad nations that take part. This was never more important than during the height of the Cold War when there was widespread mistrust between East and West. Although it will always be difficult to analyse whether the races actually helped break down these barriers, many feel that they had their part to play.

Above all, the races are about excitement, adventure and personal development for the crews, and there are not many opportunities which offer an equal challenge. There are few more demanding tasks than being woken at 3.00 a.m. when the ship is rolling violently: you hear the sound of waves breaking across the deck and you know that, after struggling into your waterproofs and safety harness, it is time for your watch to climb aloft and hand a topsail; or having to crawl up to the fore-deck and change down the jib as the wind has risen to a full gale and the bow of the yacht dips under a large green sea.

Her Majesty The Queen gave a most perceptive insight into the benefits of sail training during her presentation of the Colin Mudie-designed, 44-metre brigantine *Tunas Samudera* to the Malaysian Royal Navy on 16 October 1989:

*'Naval and commercial ships may no longer use sails for their propulsion, but the sea and the elements have not changed. Storms, tides, darkness and fog still provide a challenge to the skills and nerve of the professional seaman. There is no better way of gaining an understanding of the arts of seamanship and navigation than the experience of managing a ship under sail. Training under sail is a challenging adventure. It demands discipline, skill and knowledge and it teaches the values of teamwork and honest commitment for the sake of everyone on board. There is no room for selfishness when the lives of all on board are at stake.'*

Not only is this also true for the crews taking part in the Cutty Sark Tall Ships' Races, but they have the additional adventure of ocean racing which provides some extra dimensions to this normal experience of a sail training voyage. It gives a focus to the voyage and is a greater test of endurance for the crews. It can also enhance teamwork and sharpen the crews' skills as well offering the thrill of competition. But how did the Tall Ships' Races start and why have they grown from strength to strength since it all began in 1956?

## A Potted History

A London solicitor named Bernard Morgan had a vision of bringing the remaining windjammers together to race under sail. Racing at sea is probably as old as the art of sailing itself, but Bernard Morgan believed that this would be the last opportunity to do this as the cost of operating these ships appeared to be becoming prohibitive, and very few were being built to replace them anyway. By the autumn of 1954, the Sail Training

International Race Committee had been formed and on 7 July twenty vessels crossed the start line in Torbay and *Juana* was the first to arrive in Lisbon on the 13th. The first Tall Ships' Race had been staged.

The race was such a success that the committee was permanently established and the Articles of Association for the Sail Training Association were signed – the STA began arranging Tall Ships' Races every two years thereafter. Over the next eight years their popularity increased and an ambitious event was planned for 1964. On 24 May fifteen vessels set off from Plymouth and raced across the Atlantic to Bermuda via Lisbon. In Bermuda the fleet was joined by more vessels and they continued on a cruise-in-company to New York. That year the STA's official entry was a 52-ton yawl named *Tawau*, which was skippered by James Myatt; and amongst his afterguard were John Hamilton and Commander David Cobb – all three men were later responsible for contributing enormously to the formation of many of today's sail training organisations. John Hamilton also held the appointment of the STA Race Director of the Cutty Sark Tall Ships' Races from 1976 to 1992.

Although the 1964 event was an outstanding achievement, it raised the question of why did Britain not have a Tall Ship of her own? Inspired by the success of James Myatt's entry, a committee was set up to raise the funds and plan the building of a Tall Ship. Two years later the 300-ton topsail schooner *Sir Winston Churchill* was launched, and two years after that a sistership named *Malcolm Miller* was commissioned.

By 1972 the races had grown considerably and it was decided to seek commercial sponsorship. Up until this time the STA had been financed by wealthy individuals and many of the race expenses were borne by those who were involved in the organisation. Cutty Sark Scots Whisky sponsored the 1972 races and, with the exception of the 1979 event, have sponsored the races ever since.

1972 was not only a first for commercial sponsorship for the races, it was also the first year for the International Crew Interchange. A race series usually comprised a cruise-in-company in between two races, as indeed it does today. That year the fleet raced from the Solent to the Skaw and then cruised from Malmo to Travemunde. During the cruise the young crews had the opportunity to sail in a different ship. For example a crew member from a British 72-foot ketch would have been able to join the crew of a Scandinavian three-masted ship. The nationalities were mixed, the crews returned elated and the whole experiment was a great success. 1972 was also a truly international year as the races saw their first entry from behind the Iron Curtain. The majestic Polish full-rigged ship *Dar Pomorza* joined the 'family'. Her Polish crew were probably treated with some scepticism at first as they went ashore in large groups watched over by a 'party member'. However, their sincerity shone through and within no time at all the crews integrated within the 'family' and many friendships were formed. This process continued until the fall of the Iron Curtain in 1989. Extracts from an article by STA committee member Mrs Janka Bielak give a fascinating insight into this transition and the STA's involvement in it.

*'Poland was not a free country and my presence there could have endangered my family. I was, after all, a dirty capitalist. I missed Gdynia and instead came to assist Greville (the chairman of the Sailing Committee at that time) in Portsmouth where the STA fleet had gathered for the prize giving.*

*'The Russians were not easy; the diminutive Captain Shnider of* Kruzenshtern *kept his crew strictly incommunicado, apart from official encounters; Captain Vandenko of* Tovarishch*, as well as his officers, were also very shy. In their minds, the fact that I spoke fluent Russian placed me immediately as a spy!*

*'A KGB agent from the Soviet Embassy was present at every official reception, and the captains were never left alone. The cadets went to town only in very large groups, with a political officer inevitably in tow. They did not have any significant contact with our Western trainees.*

'The atmosphere was a little more relaxed in 1976, and Captain Shnider invited me twice for a private 'little vodka'. I got to know some of his officers, including Captains-to-be Kolomenski and Perevozchikov. In 1978, apart from Kruzenshtern – under the command of a new captain we called the Czar – we saw the first, and tiny, Russian C class entry. Sparta was skippered by Captain Chechulin and his first mate Victor Antonov (now the captain of Mir). I first met Chechulin in 1976 when he was a political officer on Tovarishch. A polyglot, who spoke English and French, he longed for acceptance as a friend, but was very much restricted by his secret duties. Nevertheless the ice was breaking, and caviar parties began to be de rigueur. The Russians adored Greville, who was such a magnificent catalyst, and the KGB reports grew increasingly favourable towards the STA.

'In 1984, Kruzenshtern entered the Cutty Sark Tall Ships' Races with Captain Kolomenski as her new master. Six class C's accompanied her. In my mind it was that year (the 1984 Jaques Cartier Race) more than any other that proved the turning point of the Russian attitude towards us. After all those years of patient work with the Russian ships, during which they were so restricted in contact with the outside world, we saw a distinct change. The two yachts, Flora (Victor Gusev) and Novik (Boris Orcechov) made an historic crossing of the Atlantic with us, becoming the first Russian yachts ever to do so. They spent six months sailing without a crew change, on a very meagre allowance and with limited food supplies. The two captains and their young trainees were fully integrated members of the STA family.

'The same year we suffered the tragic loss of the Marques. I only learned many years later, once 'perestroika' had truly set in, that Kruzenshtern's captain risked his job, and his future, by allowing his cadets to attend the memorial service in Halifax in defiance of KGB instructions.

'After 1984 every year brought good participation from the Soviet Union. All trainees and skippers have mixed freely with the rest of the STA fleet, enjoying themselves and taking part in every event. I am proud that the STA was one of the very first, link by link, to dismantle the Iron Curtain enveloping the Soviet Union. However, our efforts could not have borne fruit if it was not for the tremendous courage and unshakable perseverance of the Russian sailors in wanting to be with us. That is why I am taking my STA hat off to them.'

Janka Bielak and Captain Perevozchykov of *Sedov*. Photograph: Alexander Bielak

1973 saw the first minor race held in between the major series since 1965. The major races were held on the even years. This proved a popular addition and after another major race in 1974, there was a race during 1975 between two principal maritime festivals in Amsterdam and London.

It was decided to send the fleet across to the US to help celebrate their bicentennial in 1976. This turned out to be a milestone in the development of the races as the media were inspired by the prospect of towering masts and acres of sail lining the Hudson River on Independence Day. Five million spectators lined the banks and watched the parade of sail, and this turned out to be largest event in the bicentennial calendar.

However, media attention had been alerted a few weeks before when, tragically, two collisions occurred between the giant square-riggers at the start of the race off Bermuda. Fortunately there was no loss of life, although one crew member was seriously injured as he was caught aloft in the rigging as it collapsed all around him. There are numerous theories as to why the collisions happened, but they were probably due to a hasty decision that was made at the captains' briefing meeting in Bermuda. It was agreed to allow the ships to use their engines up to the starting gun of the race, as some captains wished to make a spectacle and set full sail before they crossed the starting line. This appeared to be going well until one ship, realising that she would arrive at the line too soon, engaged astern propulsion to slow her down. By the time the others had realised what was happening, it was too late to avoid the collisions.

The races continued to grow and develop but, with the success of the New York experience, they had changed irrevocably into major international spectator events with many principal ports queuing up to host the Tall Ships. It has been a struggle at times for the STA to resist continual pressure to commercialise the events and keep the traditional 'family' atmosphere within the races, which has been the backbone of their success. This does not mean the race series are not run in an efficient and business-like manner, but the objective has been to protect them from turning into a commercial bonanza which would undoubtedly undermine the raison d'être of the races.

In 1984 another transatlantic series was staged to mark the 450th anniversary of the voyage of Jacques Cartier who was one of the first navigators to reach Canada. This event was jointly organised by the British and American STAs. ASTA was founded by the owner and skipper of a small brigantine named *Black Pearl*. Barclay Warburton had crossed the Atlantic to participate in the 1972 race series, and was so taken with the aims and ideals of the event that he established the American association on his return.

Although the Jacques Cartier race was a tremendous achievement, it was marred by the tragic loss of the *Marques* which went down with the loss of nineteen lives. She was north of Bermuda, having started the race to Halifax the day before, and the fleet were experiencing exceptional and unpredictable winds. She was struck by a severe local squall and sailed under within two minutes. Nine crew members were rescued by the Polish schooner *Zawisza Czarny* and the Canadian frigate, and acting guard-ship, *Assinaboine*. This tragedy cast a great sadness over the fleet and the memorial service in Halifax was attended by crew members of all nationalities. The loss of the *Marques* will be remembered by all those who were racing to Halifax that night, and sympathy was extended throughout the international sail training family.

There is no doubt, and statistics confirm, that sail training and sail training races, such as the Cutty Sark Races, are relatively safe. This is because of the high standards of safety that are achieved by the individual organisations taking naval cadets to sea, or young people who have never sailed before on an adventure holiday. However, every professional who sets to sea will acknowledge that he too is at risk from the impartial elements of Mother Earth.

1985 was supposedly a 'minor year', but with 114 entries it was one of the best attended.

Thereafter the 'minor years' became major events and by 1989 even the major trophies were awarded annually. The races continued to become more widely known internationally as one of the top spectator events, and the rivalry to host the fleet became more intense. However, a port was never chosen for financial reasons, but rather because of its enthusiasm to host the event and what it could offer the young crew members. This has meant that the race circuits offered vary from an interesting array of capital cities to small harbours only just big enough to squeeze the fleet in. Word had even spread to the Antipodes, and when the Australians decided to hold a Tall Ships' Race to celebrate their bicentennial in 1988, they enlisted the expertise of the STA for advice on the planning and administration. By this time, due to the ability of their Race Director John Hamilton, the STA had developed a suite of specialist computer programmes and with their unique Rule of Rating were considered second to none in running these events.

Many of the European vessels sailed around the world to join in the Australian party, but an additional race was held in the Baltic to cater for the less adventurous. The race series continued their cycle of Baltic, Biscay, North Sea and around the British Isles, and the next transatlantic event was in 1992 to commemorate Christopher Columbus's discovery of the Americas five hundred years' before. The Columbus Regatta saw the most historic gatherings of Tall Ships in Cadiz, Puerto Rico, New York, Boston and Liverpool, and, although this was an initiative by the Spanish and Portuguese governments, the Regatta was run by a truly international committee and received the backing of technical support by the STA.

Again, an event was staged in the Baltic for all those who decided not to cross the 'pond' and join in the Columbus celebrations. This time the Tall Ships visited the independent state of Estonia for the first time, as well as Poland. It was a truly exciting time for the fleet as, after thirty-six years, one of the main aims of the Cutty Sark Tall Ships' Races had reached an historic milestone: the breaking down of barriers and promoting friendship between young people of all nations.

## The Races Today

The aims today are very much the same as before and they still focus on building international friendship within the race fleet, whilst offering an adventurous and challenging sporting event for young people. The Cutty Sark Tall Ships' Races are some of the most impressive spectator events – the numbers prove it, with over five million spectators coming to Amsterdam and Boston and two million visiting Liverpool and Newcastle. Host ports not only gain financially by the large increase in visitors, but can also benefit in other ways. In 1991 the fleet came to Belfast where 500,000 people viewed the ships over the five days. For five days a third of the community mixed freely in a carnival atmosphere. The enthusiasm and goodwill of the young crews is infectious and the visitor cannot help but absorb it. But who are the crews that sail these beautiful ships and why are the vessels so diverse and different from each other?

One of the fundamental rules for entry is that the vessel needs a waterline length of over 30 feet, which might mean that she is merely around 40 feet overall and only carries a total complement of six persons. Although this hardly fits the Tall Ship that you would imagine after reading John Masefield's poem 'I must go down to the sea again . . .', as the Australians said in 1988, 'YOU DON'T HAVE TO BE BIG TO BE TALL,' and today's fleet usually consists of many yachts and smaller craft. The crew of a smaller vessel in the fleet gains just as much as the cadets in a lofty square-rigger and contributes equally to the success of the event.

The ships are divided into three classes. In Class A are up to ten or so of the largest square-riggers afloat today, each holding a crew of around 300. Class B consists of the medium-sized ships: usually numbering about twenty-five, roughly the size of the British 300-ton topsail schooner *Sir Winston Churchill*. The remaining vessels are divided into three divisions in Class C, with the modern yachts which fly spinnakers being grouped together.

The large square-riggers in the fleet are generally state-owned and operated, and train cadets for a future in their respective navies. These need to be state run and financed as the cost of operating one of these giants can be in excess of £5,000 a day. The cadets are usually on board for a three-month period and, amongst many other subjects, will learn the arts of seamanship, navigation and leadership. These beautiful ships and their crews also serve as ambassadors for their country – there are few more impressive sights than a square-rigger in a port on a state visit.

The smaller vessels mainly carry young people who are on board for a few weeks to experience the challenges and fun of an adventure holiday. These yachts and traditional craft normally operate throughout the sailing season and the Cutty Sark Races are often considered the highlight of the year. A converted Danish fishing boat built in 1989 takes just as much teamwork to sail efficiently as a state-of-the-art ocean racer and, because of the STA Rule of Rating, each has an equal chance of winning.

Although the main prize, the Cutty Sark Trophy, is awarded to the vessel which, in the opinion of the participants, has contributed the most towards international understanding and friendship, the racing is still a vital element. Whilst the crews are at sea, they put immense effort into keeping their ship ahead of their nearest rivals, and there have been many nail biting races where vessels have crossed the finish line within seconds of each other after days at sea. But when the ships arrive in port and the spontaneous parties begin, stories and experiences are shared, friendships are formed and rivalries are forgotten.

So the vision of one man has manifested itself into one of the greatest spectator events of today thanks to the tireless dedication of many characters. The international 'family' continues to grow and is the key to the future of the races. The Sail Training Association endures to keep its specialist technical expertise and experience and is widely acknowledged as being second to none when it comes to organising Tall Ships' Races, and Cutty Sark Scots Whisky continues to provide the sponsorship to enable it all to happen.

## The Future – Tall Ships 2000

An event is being planned by the STA to organise a global Tall Ships' Race to celebrate the bi-millennium. This will be centred around the North Atlantic basin, and a conventional course has been chosen to take advantage of the prevailing currents and winds. There will also be a number of events in the Pacific and the Antipodes. There are many major cities which have an established track record of hosting the Tall Ships like Amsterdam, Bremerhaven and Boston – these ports have undoubtedly realised the benefits of hosting the fleet. They have the funding and ambassadorial power to attract the state ships and will continue to feature strongly in the future.

However, there is a dark cloud on the horizon. Because of the breakdown in the economies of Eastern Europe, more Academies are finding it immensely difficult to finance their large ships. Some have resorted to sponsorship, and others are working with agents and are taking on fare paying passengers. Although sponsorship can result in a brilliant symbiotic relationship when working well, these ships will be vulnerable to commercial exploitation which could begin to undermine the ethos of the races. Apart from this, the future looks bright with the exciting series to look forward to and the traditional Cutty Sark Races continuing to grow in popularity every year.

# THE STA RULE OF RATING – THE BEST KEPT SECRET

How can a traditional Danish gaff-rigged fishing boat built in 1895 ever compete with the state-of-the-art maxi ocean-racer built of exotic materials? How can the largest square-rigger in commision today of over 3,000 tons, race together with either of these craft and stand an equal chance of winning? It is all due to the magic STA Rule of Rating.

In fact it is not so much magic, but more of a mathematical formula which has been refined and developed since the races began. Its success is due to the fact that it has been kept a secret; only known to the few who have been instrumental in its development. Therefore no competitor has been able to exploit any loopholes that there might be.

A rule of rating is not the same as a handicap system, which is used in a lot of other sailing races and has a subjective human interpretation. A vessel's 'form' or recorded performance will be taken directly into account with a handicap system, whereas a rule of rating relies purely on a set of dimensions and other relevant data being fed into a formula to give a Time Correction Factor (TCF). In round terms the slowest vessel in a Cutty Sark fleet has a TCF of .500 and the fastest yacht would have a TCF of just over 1.000. This figure is simply multiplied to a vessel's Elapsed Time (Real Time) which produces its Corrected Time and this is how the slowest vessel can theoretically win the race on Corrected Time. For example, if the slowest vessel takes 4 days 12 hours to complete the course and the fastest takes 2 days 7 hours to finish, the slower vessel would win by 1 hour (108 hrs x .500 = 54 hrs, against 55 hrs x 1.000 = 55 hrs).

A rule of rating is not an uncommon way of administering sailing races, but what is unusual in a Cutty Sark Tall Ships' Race is that a vessel which does not cross the finishing line before the time limit can also win. A crew of a small, but heavy, traditional vessel might have sailed more skilfully and have worked harder than a crew of an ultra-light displacement yacht which was first to cross the line. It would be unfair to disqualify the slower yacht for not finishing the race because of the light winds that prevailed. Therefore, by means of a formula, the slower vessel's distance can be calculated to give an estimated time which can be included in the race results.

Measuring a vessel for the races, and ensuring that the measurements which have been submitted are as accurate as possible, has always posed a problem. In the beginning, especially when communications were difficult with the Eastern block countries, the data received was sometimes ambiguous, and other times obviously incorrect. Once, when a large square-rigger arrived and anchored off Tenerife, an ingenious race official resorted to using a sextant in order to calculate the maximum height of its mast! With more efficient means of communication (telex, fax and E-mail) the data has become more accurate and, therefore, it is possible to match the fleet's performance more exactly.

The STA Rule of Rating has been remarkably successful in allowing such a diverse racing fleet to compete on an equal footing, and is in itself part of a winning formula which does so much to foster friendship each year amongst a truly international fleet.

# THE ROUTES OF THE CUTTY SARK TALL SHIPS' RACES

Planning the routes the ships take every year on these international races all begins with a pattern which has emerged since the races began in 1956.

The first race, although it was well supported by north European and Scandinavian ships, was across the Bay of Biscay. This was an ideal area to hold a race series as the large sailing ships enjoyed good sailing, relatively unimpeded by other shipping and with few navigational hazards. It also presented a real challenge to the smaller vessels and was very popular because of the warm climate.

In 1958 the course was very similar, racing from Brest to Spain and the Canaries. 1960 saw the fleet in the Mediterranean but, although the climate was agreeable, the winds were typically fickle and unpredictable. There are not as many true sail training vessels based in the Mediterranean and it was a long way for the north European ships to go to reach the start. This is why the races have not been held there often.

By the end of the 1960s, the decade had seen the race series venturing up to Scandinavia and northern Europe and, although the North Sea is encumbered with navigational obstacles, these races were also popular as most of the participants had less distance to travel to join the start. In 1964, the first transatlantic Tall Ships' Race was concluded, and on average they have been repeated about every eight or ten years since. In 1965 a minor event was staged in between the major races which, until then, were only held in the 'even' years.

The 1970s saw the fleet racing into the Baltic for the first time, which captured the imagination of the Scandinavians, and, because of the large number of sail training ships that are based there, it became a popular venue. There were a number of minor races held up in the Firth of Clyde but support for these dwindled after 1977.

The current pattern emerged during the 1980s and has more or less continued ever since. In general terms there is a Baltic series which might be followed by one in the North Sea and then by a race across the Bay of Biscay. This is interspersed by a transatlantic series, and by one which is set in a different area like the 'Leek, Shamrock, Thistle and Tulip' series in 1991.

Within this framework other trends have established themselves, like Sail Amsterdam which is generally held every fifth year. There have also been a few independent international gatherings of Tall Ships, like the celebrations surrounding the centenary of the Statue of Liberty in New York during 1986, but the first major sail training event outside the usual pattern was in 1988 when the Sail Training Association acted as consultants for the Australian Bicentennial Authority for their celebrations. Since then STA support has been sought for all other major sail training events, like the planned future series in Indonesia, Japan and Australia.

A series is usually decided on four years before it is due to start and the successful ports will have been through a bidding process at the STA International Conference which is held each autumn. The port will have needed to prove it can provide the fleet with good mooring facilities and an appropriate infrastructure of support services for the ships and their crews. They will also have had to have submitted an excellent social programme for the trainees, to ensure that they have a memorable time mixing together and sharing their experiences.

A successful port will have to put substantial resources behind the event but will recoup them indirectly by the influx of large numbers of visitors, media coverage and prestige. This is why there is no shortage of ports, large and small, registering to hold the event. The actual process of selecting a port is simple; the STA International Racing Committee will make a decision based on the views of the captains and operators of the ships. Cutty Sark Scots

Whisky, the event sponsor, will have limited influence on the decision as they are aware of the importance of the route being chosen by those who participate.

The smaller ports are often more successful at holding an event than the major ports, as it is easier to ensure that the event does not become too commercial and contributes little to fostering international understanding and friendship amongst the crews. However, many capital cities, like Stockholm, have managed to achieve the happy balance of providing the crews with excellent facilities whilst benefitting from the considerable number of spectators the event attracts.

The successful port will also need to be situated in the right geographical location as a race leg is generally about 400 to 600 miles long. After the first race leg of the series, there will usually be a cruise-in-company of about 200 miles and then another race leg of between 400 to 600 miles.

This procedure of deciding the route of a Cutty Sark Tall Ships' Race also has to take into account the world's 'political' agenda, as the state-owned ships are often directed towards various national celebrations and commemorations.

The successful pattern which has emerged offers variety to those who compete regularly. It spreads a popular international event around, so that many millions of people can enjoy the experience of viewing these majestic vessels competing against each other and the spectacle and romance of the fleet moored in harbour. More importantly, they witness thousands of young people from many different nations mixing together in a unique environment.

Photograph overleaf: Janka Bielak

# THE CUTTY SARK TROPHY

The trophy is presented by the race sponsors and the beautifully crafted silver replica of the most famous clipper, the *Cutty Sark*, has epitomised the races since its introduction in 1974. It is awarded annually to the vessel which, in the opinion of the captains and crews who participate, has contributed the most towards fostering international understanding and friendship during the race series.

As a captain, it is often a tall order to cast your vote, even after taking advice from your crew members, as there are usually many crews which have added considerably to the 'family' atmosphere and goodwill which exists during the races. However, a ship and her crew may have done something outstanding to secure the trophy, as was the case in 1976 when the Belgian vessel *Zenobe Gramme* towed *Kukri* and *Erika* for over 800 miles to Bermuda after the fleet experienced unusually light winds and their provisions were running low. Two years earlier saw the first entry from the USSR in the form of the second largest square-rigger afloat, *Kruzenshtern*. This marked a giant leap forward for international understanding and friendship and was recognised by the award of the trophy to her.

Cutty Sark Scots Whisky

The previous winning crews have come from many countries, and their vessels have ranged from the smallest to the largest in the fleet. They have consisted of cadets bound for a career in their navy as well as teams of young people with little sailing experience. The crews have been all men, mixed, or all women. The one thing they have in common is that they have all been part of a winning team which has won one of the most internationally coveted trophies.

| 1974 | *Kruzenshtern* | USSR | 1986 | *Atlantica* | Sweden |
| 1976 | *Zenobe Gramme* | Belgium | 1988 | *Urania* | Netherlands |
| 1978 | *Gladan* | Sweden | 1990 | *Jens Krogh* | Denmark |
| 1980 | *Dar Pomorza* | Poland | 1991 | *Asgard II* | Ireland |
| 1982 | *Urania* | Netherlands | 1992 | *Gladan* | Sweden |
| 1984 | *Sir Winston Churchill* | UK | 1993 | *Colin Archer* | Norway |

The original clipper, on which the trophy is modelled, was named after the witch in Robert Burns's epic poem 'Tam O'Shanter', written in 1790. The story recounts farmer Tam riding home one dark and stormy night when he had the misfortune to come across a coven of witches. He spied on one very attractive witch wearing only a 'cutty sark', (which translates from old Scots into 'short shirt'). Realising that Tam was spying on her, 'Cutty Sark' pursued him at great speed snatching his horse's tail as Tam escaped with his life by crossing running water (this is something a witch cannot do).

The original tea clipper lived up to her speedy namesake by completing many fast passages, bringing home firstly tea from China and latterly wool from Australia. After a successful passage, the crew would place a braided piece of rope, signifying a mare's tail, in the outstretched hand of the fine figurehead of the witch. Although, when she was built in 1869, tea clippers were only expected to have an average working life of ten years, *Cutty Sark* was working until the 1920s before she was finally restored and put into dry dock as a museum ship at Greenwich in 1957.

Meanwhile, the wine and spirit merchants Berry Bros & Rudd were planning in 1923 to launch their new, high quality Scots whisky on the export market and invited the famous artist James McBey to design the label. He suggested the name 'Cutty Sark' and sketched the famous design of the clipper under full sail. Since then the Scots whisky has become as famous throughout the world as the clipper ever was, and thus Berry Bros & Rudd have supported the races since 1972.

# THE BOSTON TEAPOT TROPHY

The story of the Boston Teapot started in 1964, after the transatlantic Tall Ships' Race to America. Two vessels were sailing back from Boston to Europe, and one of them would benefit financially from their sponsors if she were taking part in a race, or other competition. It was decided that some form of trophy would be awarded for the fastest passage, greatest noon to noon run, or other feat. The details were not worked out until after the vessels had sailed, but it was decided that the trophy should be called 'The Boston Teapot'.

Brooke Bond Tea obtained permission from the Boston Fine Arts Museum to copy a silver teapot which was in use at Boston at the time of 'The Tea Party'. The Tea Party was the act of renuciation that presaged the American War of Independence and was described as 'bold, daring, firm, intrepid and inflexible' by the second President of the United States. The trophy now serves as a testament to the principles on which the Sail Training Association was founded.

The trophy is awarded to the sail training vessel which has covered the greatest distance in any period of 124 hours. How this period of 124 hours was established can only be described as something curiously British, but it has not stopped vessels vigorously competing for the trophy since its inception.

The past winners have been:

| Year | Vessel | Nation | Distance | Average Speed |
|------|--------|--------|----------|---------------|
| 1964 | Corsaro II | Italy | 1121 | 9.04ks |
| 1965 | Gorch Fock | Germany | 1079 | 8.70 |
| 1966 | Libertad | Argentina | 1335 | 10.77 |
| 1967 | Gorch Fock | Germany | 1040 | 8.39 |
| 1968 | Gorch Fock | Germany | | |
| 1969 | Gorch Fock | Germany | 1191 | 9.60 |
| 1970 | Gloria | Colombia | 1058 | 8.53 |
| 1971 | Esmeralda | Chile | 1026 | 8.27 |
| 1972 | Eagle | USA | 1100 | 8.87 |
| 1973 | Eagle | USA | 1019 | 8.22 |
| 1974 | Juan Sebastian de Elcano | Spain | 952 | 7.68 |
| 1976 | Libertad | Argentina | 1248 | 10.06 |
| 1977 | Juan Sebastian de Elcano | Spain | 1029 | 8.30 |
| 1982 | Libertad | Argentina | 1115 | 8.99 |
| 1983 | Cisne Branco | Chile | 1101 | 8.88 |
| 1984 | Gorch Fock | Germany | 1098 | 8.85 |
| 1986 | Nippon Maru | Japan | 955 | 7.70 |
| 1987 | Libertad | Argentina | 1174 | 9.47 |
| 1988 | Libertad | Argentina | 1206 | 9.73 |
| 1989 | Nippon Maru | Japan | 1134 | 9.15 |
| 1990 | Kaiwo Maru | Japan | 1340 | 10.81 |
| 1991 | Kaiwo Maru | Japan | 1244 | 10.03 |
| 1992 | Libertad | Argentina | 1040 | 8.39 |
| 1993 | Nippon Maru | Japan | 1201 | 9.69 |

# OTHER TROPHIES AND AWARDS

## The Ince Trophy

The Ince Trophy can be competed for by any sail training vessel of any nation provided that she is between 11 and 30.5 metres and she complies with the STA's Racing and Sailing Regulations. It is presented annually to the vessel which has covered the greatest Corrected Distance in any period of thirty-six hours. The Corrected Distance is calculated by dividing the distance that she has covered by her Time Correction Factor.

The past winners have been:

| | | |
|---|---|---|
| 1969 Zulu | 1973 Asgard | 1978 St Barbara III |
| 1970 Zulu | 1974 St Barbara III | 1981 Sir Thomas Sopwith |
| 1971 Zulu | 1975 Sir Thomas Sopwith | 1982 Jolie Brise |
| 1972 Asgard | 1977 Mistral | 1990 Duet |

## The Cape Horn Trophy

The Cape Horn Trophy is awarded annually to the ship which finishes first on Corrected Time in Class A. This trophy consists of a real piece of rock brought back from Cape Horn and has been won by some of the most prestigious sail training ships in the world.

## The Crowther Memorial Shield

The Crowther Memorial Shield was commissioned and presented to *Rona* by Robert Crowther who sadly lost his son when the light aircraft in which he was flying crashed at the start of the race off Fowey in 1979. The crew of *Rona* showed outstanding bravery and courage when they tried to save those in the plane.

It has since been appropriately awarded annually to the vessel which has been involved with an act of safety at sea. *Ocean Venture*'s assistance in the rescue of a French yacht and her crew racing in the 1987 Fastnet Race is a more recent example of this.

## The Florence Cup

This giant silver cup is presented during every race series to the ship which finishes first in Class B on Corrected Time. The fast Swedish schooners *Falken* and *Gladan* often win this award.

## The Greville Howard Memorial Shield

This award was inaugurated in 1989 in memory of Commander the Hon. Greville Howard who was affectionately known as the 'father' of the fleet. Greville contributed enormously to the international reputation of the races and was a man of cast iron principles which permeated throughout the 'family'. He is sadly missed, but this fitting memorial is awarded to the vessel which has contributed the most towards the international crew interchange every year.

## The Reith Memorial Plate

This beautiful silver plate was commissioned in memory of Hans Reith who was the ubiquitous owner of the gaff ketch *Carola* which participated in many Cutty Sark Races. It is awarded annually to a vessel which has suffered particular hardship during the series.

## The Helmut Bastian Bell

This trophy was donated by STA Germany in 1972 for the vessel with the highest proportion of young trainees on board. Helmut Bastian was a keen ocean racing captain as well as chairman of the Hamburg sited, German open-sea sporting society HANSA and head of a Bremen shipping company.

## The Honorary Company of Master Mariners Award

This perpetual trophy is presented to the vessel which has shown outstanding seamanship during the races, quite often in connection with a gear failure which may have occurred.

## The Vicky Scott Memorial Prize

After every race series the captain of the winning square-rigged ship on Corrected Time is presented with a beautifully engraved decanter in memory of Vicky Scott, the late wife of Morin Scott, who was instrumental in the creation of *Royalist*.

## The Royal Thames Yacht Club Challenge Cup

This graceful silver bowl was first donated at the end of the first race series in 1956 as a general award, but from 1993 it will be presented at the STA Annual Conference to the 'newcomer' which has contributed the most towards the race series.

## The Shipping Federation of Great Britain Perpetual Trophy

This trophy was reintroduced in 1993 to be presented at the STA Annual Conference to the vessel which has shown greatest loyalty to the races.

# THE
# TALL SHIPS

Photographs opposite and above: Cutty Sark Scots Whisky

# LIBERTAD

This majestic flush-decked, full-rigged ship is one of the fastest windjammers afloat today. Her record breaking transatlantic run in 1966, from Cape Rice in Canada to Burcey Island off Ireland, was completed in 6 days 21 hours at an average speed of 10.5 knots. During this remarkable passage she averaged 18 knots at times, which is comparable to the state-of-the-art Whitbread Round the World yachts of today – who needs water ballast, gorillas, kevlar and other exotic materials!

She has also won the much-coveted Boston Teapot Trophy more times than any other vessel, covering as much as 1,335 nautical miles within 124 hours. Ironically, she lodged her entry form and won this trophy in the same year as the outbreak of the Falklands War, which emphasises how politics are often kept out of the international world of sail training.

Built by the Rio Santiago Naval Shipyard, she was launched in 1956, but only commissioned in 1960. She replaced her full-rigged predecessor *President Sarmiento*, which was built at the famous Camel Laird Yard in Birkenhead in 1897. This ship was named after the President, Domingo Faustino Sarmiento, who was instrumental in building up the Argentine navy.

Apart from being one of the largest square-rigged ships, she is distinctive by her forward wheel-house bridge which breaks her flush deck. Her first Tall Ships' Race was in 1964 when she joined the transatlantic fleet and she has participated in all subsequent transatlantic races since (1976, 1984 and 1992).

## DATA

| | |
|---|---|
| Year built: 1956 | Sail area: 2,655.4m² |
| Rig: Full-rigged ship | Tonnage: 4,092 grt; 3,750 |
| Max length: 102.6m | Crew complement: 315 |
| Length of hull: 90.9m | Owner: Argentinian Navy |
| Max height: 59.1m | Construction: Steel |
| Beam: 13.7m | Builder: Rio Santiago Naval Shipyard, Argentina |
| Draught: 7.0m | Engine: 2 x diesel, 2,400 total b.h.p. |

Photograph: Janka Bielak

# LEEUWIN

This elegant, blue-hulled barquentine is named after the famous Dutch vessel which, in 1622, was the first to round the south-western point of the Australian continent. Both the ship and the cape bear the Dutch name for 'lioness'.

The international success of Alan Bond's 1983 victory in the America's Cup significantly helped the STA of Western Australia and various other groups to raise the finance necessary to build this fine ship. The Australian Bicentennial Authority also gave a generous grant to ensure that she would be ready to compete in the 1988 celebrations.

She first went to sea on 12 September 1986 to host spectators when Australia defended the America's Cup, but started her sail training programme in May 1987. Her programme has been developed since then and she now operates an excellent system where, towards the end of the voyage, her trainees take over the running of the vessel. The voyage crew nominate their stand-in captain and watch leaders, and the permanent crew only advise if they are at risk of putting themselves or the ship in danger. This obviously develops qualities of responsibility, discipline and confidence whilst providing a long-lasting sense of achievement.

## DATA

Year built: 1986
Rig: Barquentine
Max length: 52.1m
Length of hull: 41.3m
Max height: 32.3m
Beam: 9.0m
Draught: 3.5m

Sail area: 781.6m²
Tonnage: 236 grt; 300 displacement; 99 net
Crew complement: 53
Owner: Leeuwin Sail Training Foundation Ltd.
Construction: Steel
Builder: Australian Shipbuilding Industries Ltd, Western Australia
Engine: 2 x 230 b.h.p. Detroit Straight 6, diesel

Photograph: Janka Bielak

# YOUNG ENDEAVOUR

In 1988, on a bright sunny Australia Day, this beautiful brigantine was ceremonially handed over to the government of Australia by H.R.H. The Prince of Wales. Her glistening topsides were painted in the same distinctive blue that is used on Her Majesty's yacht *Britannia*, and, despite being sailed halfway around the world, she looked immaculate. This bicentennial present had been the brainchild of Mr Arthur Weller and was financed by British industry and Mr Weller personally.

She started her adventurous voyage from Britain in August 1987 and was skilfully sailed to Sydney by a selected Australian and British crew. The selections had taken place during the previous winter and the twelve British crew were chosen from over 2,500 young people.

The voyage was a great success and the Colin Mudie designed ship had proved herself as an excellent sail training vessel. In the Tall Ships' Race from Hobart to Sydney, she won her class and almost won overall with the internationally renowned sail training Captain Chris Blake in command. Since 1988, she has been operated by the Australian navy, taking young civilians for voyages around the Australian coast and sometimes further afield.

She joined the enormous Columbus Regatta fleet in 1992 with an Australian crew, and returned to complete her circumnavigation later that year.

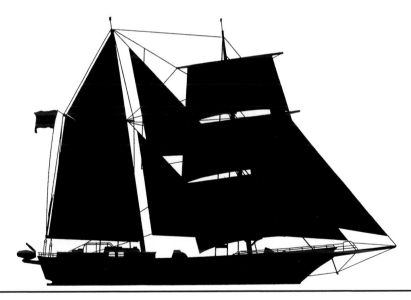

## DATA

| | |
|---|---|
| Year built: 1987 | Sail area: 649.1m² |
| Rig: Brigantine | Tonnage: 175 grt; 239 displacement |
| Max length: 42.1m | Crew complement: 37 |
| Length of hull: 34.9m | Owner: Australian Federal Government |
| Max height: 30.7m | Construction: Steel |
| Beam: 7.9m | Builder: Brooke Yachts, Lowestoft, UK |
| Draught: 3.7m | Engine: 2 x Perkins V8 185 b.h.p. diesel |

Photograph: Janka Bielak

# KALIAKRA

This Bulgarian state ship made her Cutty Sark Tall Ships' Race début in 1986 with an impressively fast passage across the North Sea from Newcastle to Bremerhaven. She was just 'pipped at the post' by the London Sailing Project's *Donald Searle*, which took line honours. However, she did beat the famous, round-the-world maxi *Great Britain II*, which was being crewed by the Royal Navy Reserves, and many other prestigious racing yachts.

Since then, her arch rival has become her sistership *ORP Iskra II* which is operated by the Polish Navy. *ORP Iskra II* was built two years before her Bulgarian sister and differs in having a vertical transom, a clearer deck with less deckhouses and an open bridge deck. These vessels spar together during most Cutty Sark Tall Ships' Races, although *Kaliakra* appears to have the edge since her rig was altered in 1989. Her foremast was extended so that it is now level with her main mast which enables her to carry a royal and an extra headsail. She also has two other sisters, *Pogoria* and *Oceania*. The Bulgarian Merchant Navy has trained its cadets and officers since 1879 with six other vessels but this *Kaliakra* also takes young men from the Bulgarian navy and various youth organisations. Her friendly crews have always been quick to integrate well within the 'family' during the many Cutty Sark Tall Ships' Races that she has taken part in, and she has earned the reputation of becoming one of the most popular vessels in the fleet. When she is not racing she is to be found sail training in the Black Sea.

## DATA

| | |
|---|---|
| Year built: 1984 | Sail area: 990.5m² |
| Rig: Barquentine | Tonnage: 247 grt |
| Max length: 48.4m | Crew complement: 51 |
| Length of hull: 42.8m | Owner: Navigation Maritime Bulgare |
| Max height: 33.1m | Construction: Steel; teak-laid decks |
| Beam: 8.0m | Builder: Lenin Shipyard, Gdansk, Poland |
| Draught: 3.5m | Engine: 310 b.h.p. diesel |

Photograph: Janka Bielak

# ESMERALDA

The pretty name *Esmeralda* has been associated with the Chilean navy since the blockade of the port of Valparaiso during the war of independence in 1818. She is the sixth Chilean naval ship to bear this name; her predecessors include a light cruiser, one of the most powerful warships of her time, and an anti-submarine frigate.

Her virtual sistership *Juan Sebastian de Elcano* was built in 1927 and also designed by the famous English Camper and Nicholson yacht designers. Both ships were built in Cadiz by Echevarrieta y Larriñaga, but *Esmeralda's* keel was laid down in the name of *Jual de Austria* for the Spanish navy in 1942. During her build she was almost devastated by fire, but in 1951 she was sold to the Chilean government and was launched in 1952 after a rebuild.

She is rigged as a barquentine, making her different from *Juan Sebastian de Elcano* which is a topsail schooner (she has no fore and aft rig on the foremast). She also has an extended fo'c's'le which runs back unbroken to the main mast, whereas *Juan Sebastian de Elcano's* fo'c's'le is conventional and dips by the foremast. Both ships also have a novel exhaust system for their 1,500 b.h.p. diesel engines which runs neatly up the lower jigger mast.

*Esmeralda* has competed in the majority of the main Tall Ships' gatherings, taking part in the 1964 and 1976 Operation Sails in New York, the Osaka Sea Festival in 1983 and the celebrations in 1986 to commemorate the centenary of the Statue of Liberty. She has also taken part in the Columbus Regatta in 1992 as well as some intervening Cutty Sark Tall Ships' Races.

She operates a busy schedule training young officers and cadets of the Chilean navy, crossing the vast oceans of the world.

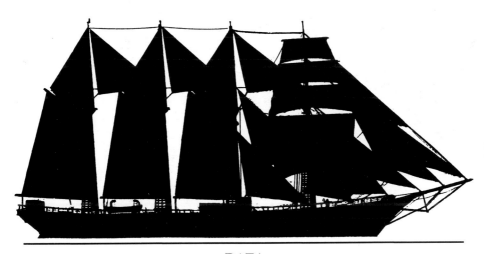

## DATA

| | |
|---|---|
| Year built: 1952 | Sail area: 2,373.7m² |
| Rig: 4-masted barquentine | Tonnage: 3,222 displacement |
| Max length: 106.6m | Crew complement: 328 |
| Length of hull: 92.6m | Owner: Chilean Navy |
| Max height: 49.1m | Construction: Steel |
| Beam: 13.4m | Builder: Echevarrieta y Larriñaga, Cadiz, Spain |
| Draught: 6.9m | Engine: 1,500 b.h.p., Fiat, diesel |

Photograph: Janka Bielak

# GLORIA

The South American countries are well represented with state ships which have dual roles – to train the naval cadets and to represent their nation wherever they visit. Argentina, Chile, Uruguay, Venezuela, Ecuador and Mexico all have ships, and many have evolved from the 1983 design of Blohm and Voss, the *Tovarishch* class. *Gloria* like her sistership *Guayas*, differs by being some fifty feet shorter and by her pronounced bridge and wheelhouse at the forward end of her poop deck. Although this is not conventional, and perhaps spoils the traditional lines of a ship, it does offer a protected position to helm by. This has obvious benefits when encountering severe weather on her world cruises.

*Gloria* has participated in the Cutty Sark Races and gatherings and first entered in the 1972 series. She has covered many miles since she was launched in 1968 (on one voyage via Australia and South Africa she sailed over 27,000 miles) and is specifically designed to stay at sea for sixty days without replenishing. She is not only well designed to carry out these global adventures, but also has a museum on board displaying Colombian artifacts to complement her role as ambassador.

## DATA

| | |
|---|---|
| Year built: 1968 | Sail area: 1,073.3m² |
| Rig: Barque | Crew complement: 132 |
| Max length: 74.2m | Owner: Colombian Navy |
| Length of hull: 64.6m | Construction: Steel |
| Max height: 39.64m | Builder: Sener Sistemas Marinos SA, Madrid, Spain |
| Beam: 10.6m | Engine: 530 b.h.p. diesel |
| Draught: 4.4m | |

Photograph: Janka Bielak

# DANMARK

Denmark has one of the oldest traditions in sail training which started when King Christian IV (1588–1648) sent the sloop *Den Dynkerker Bojert* on a training cruise. Since then Denmark has had many ships actively engaged in training, which include two named *Georg Stage* and the beautiful four-masted barque named *Viking* which was built in 1907 and is now afloat (but no longer sailing) in Gothenburg.

The great five-masted barque *Kobenhaven* took over the role from *Viking* of training Danish cadets, but tragically she was lost with all hands in 1928 on a voyage from Buenos Aires to Melbourne. Very few five-masted barques were built and all were lost at sea. Some experts believe the immense spread of canvas would have been unmanageable for the crew if the ship was struck by a freak squall 'all standing'. After this disaster, the Danish government stepped in and assumed responsibility for training their seamen, which resulted in *Danmark* being built in 1933 after a parliamentary decision. Until the war she would take 120 boys on a seven-month cruise every year. Fortunately *Danmark* had visited the New York World Fair and, at the outbreak of war, was taken to Jacksonville in Florida, where she was handed over to the US Coastguard by Captain Hansen. 5,000 cadets were trained during the war and most of her original Danish crew joined the Allied war effort. Remarkably, seven captained their own vessels before the age of twenty-one.

Captain Hansen went on to command *Danmark* over the years, through her major refit in 1959 when she was modernised considerably, until he retired in 1964. He was a highly respected square-rigger master, both by the other captains and by those who served under him.

Until her next major refit in 1990, she operated two long voyages per year and her trainees spent five months aboard learning the values of living at sea and undergoing training in basic seamanship. Her busy schedule has now been reduced to one major voyage a year, but she continues to keep her tradition of participating in some Tall Ships' gatherings. She represented her country as their flagship in the 1992 Columbus Regatta.

## DATA

| | |
|---|---|
| Year built: 1933 | Sail area: 1,623.3m² |
| Rig: Full-rigged Ship | Tonnage: 790 grt; 845 tm |
| Max length: 73.9m | Crew complement: 99 |
| Length of hull: 64.7m | Owner: Danish Government |
| Max height: 37.7m | Construction: Steel |
| Beam: 10.0m | Builder: Nakskov Shipyard, Lolland, Denmark |
| Draught: 4.5m | Engine: 486 b.h.p. Frichs, diesel |

Photograph: Janka Bielak

# GEORG STAGE

To many discerning eyes *Georg Stage* is the prettiest of all ships sailing today. One of the smaller full-rigged ships, this delightful vessel and her young crews have always been excellent ambassadors for their country. She can sometimes be spotted in port during a Cutty Sark Tall Ships' Race with lines of dark blue uniforms hanging in the rigging, drying in the breeze.

The original *Georg Stage* (now preserved as a museum ship at Mystic Seaport, Connecticut) was donated by the Danish shipowner Carl Frederik Stage and his wife Thea to the 'Georg Stage Minde', in memory of their son who sadly died at the age of twenty-one. They later bequeathed a sum of money to support the ship's operation.

Her replacement was constructed during 1934/5 and started her first voyage in April 1935. The cadets traditionally apply for a berth in January and February and are selected from all walks of life to start their voyage on 20 April. To apply, they need to be between sixteen and twenty years' old and in perfect health having shown good behaviour whilst at school. Initially their training focuses on safety and working aloft in sheltered bays and anchoring at night. After a month their seamanship training extends to open waters in the Baltic, and instruction is also given in signalling, navigation, maintenance, first aid, physics, mathematics, Danish and English. Thereafter, they will cross the North Sea or enter a Cutty Sark Tall Ships' Race and complete their sail training voyage on 20 September in Copenhagen. The trainees will then help with her annual refit whilst looking for a job and, by October, most will have found suitable positions at sea. Her professional crew consists of a captain and four officers. The purser also acts as engineer, communications officer and chief steward.

This highly successful organisation is headed by a board of ten voluntary members who are in one way or another connected with shipping or the Royal Danish Navy. The operation is funded by the Stage legacy, sponsorship from companies and the Danish government (unlike the British government which provides no direct funding to the British organisations).

## DATA

| | |
|---|---|
| Year built: 1935 | Sail area: 871.5m² |
| Rig: Full-rigged ship | Tonnage: 298 grt |
| Max length: 51.2m | Crew complement: 71 |
| Length of hull: 42.0m | Owner: Stiftlesen Georg Stage Minde |
| Max height: 29.2m | Construction: Steel |
| Beam: 8.5m | Builder: Frederikshavn Shipyard, Denmark |
| Draught: 3.7m | Engine: 220 b.h.p. diesel |

Photograph: Janka Bielak

# JENS KROGH

*Jens Krogh* was designed as a Danish fishing boat and worked the Kattegat and North Sea until 1957. She originally had a 6 b.h.p. auxiliary engine, and a well in the middle of the hull which was open to the sea and allowed the fish to remain alive until harbour was reached. She was built in 1899 at the H.V. Buhl Shipyard in Frederikshavn, which makes her one of the oldest participants in the Cutty Sark Tall Ships' Races today. In 1912 she was registered in Esbjerg under the name of *Ida*, and later she was re-registered in Grena and Saeby where her name was changed to *Ulla Vita*.

In 1973 she was bought by a youth organisation in Aalborg which has similar aims to the British Sea Scouts. After a major three-year restoration, which was mainly carried out by the volunteer members of the FDF/FPF Aalborg Sokreds, she was put into operation and has continued to take many young crews to sea every year.

In 1982 she entered the Cutty Sark Tall Ships' Race from Falmouth to Lisbon. That year *Jens Krogh* and the fleet continued on to Vigo in a cruise-in-company and raced back to Southampton. The skipper was Bo Rosbjerg who was one of the leading lights in the project and is now the STA's Danish national representative. Since then Bo and his team have entered many races and were awarded the Cutty Sark Trophy in 1990. In 1992 they took on the mammoth task of entering a vessel in the Columbus Regatta and achieved one of the top placings in the race from Cadiz to Puerto Rico.

This Danish youth organisation is one of the key members of the international 'family' as well as being an excellent ambassador for its country.

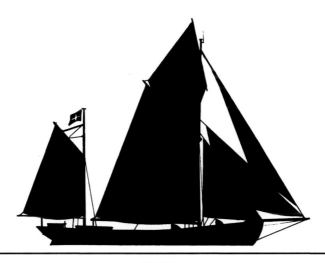

## DATA

| | |
|---|---|
| Year built: 1899 | Sail area: 206.9m² |
| Rig: Gaff ketch | Tonnage: 50 displacement (approx) |
| Max length: 23.8m | Crew complement: 15 |
| Length of hull: 18.6m | Owner: FDF/FPF Aalborg Sokreds |
| Max height: 21.0m | Construction: Wood |
| Beam: 4.9m | Builder: H.V. Buhl Shipyard, Frederikshavn, Denmark |
| Draught: 2.2m | |

Photograph: Cutty Sark Scots Whisky

# GUAYAS

A magnificent figurehead of a giant condor in full flight distinguishes *Guayas* from her Colombian sistership *Gloria*. She also differs by her open upper bridge instead of an enclosed wheelhouse. Both ships were built at the same Spanish shipyard in Bilbao and are forerunners of their larger stablemates *Simon Bolivar* and the Mexican ship *Cuauhtemoc*.

Named after the river on which the Ecuadorian Naval Superior School is situated, she has been taking cadets from this college since she was launched in 1976. The school was founded by the legendary liberator of South America, Simon Bolivar, and since 1822 has a history of training youngsters bound for a naval career.

She has represented Ecuador throughout the world, participating in many of the Cutty Sark Tall Ships' Races. She also participated in the Australian bicentennial celebrations in 1988 as well as in the 1986 Statue of Liberty celebrations in New York. She is a well-proven sail training ship, having sailed extensively in many of the world's oceans, including the Pacific.

Her crew have always been great ambassadors for their country and can quite often be seen parading in the streets dancing to Latin American music played by their on-board band.

## DATA

| | |
|---|---|
| Year built: 1976 | Sail area: 1,886.5m² |
| Rig: Barque | Tonnage: 934 grt |
| Max length: 79.5m | Crew complement: 175 |
| Length of hull: 64.5m | Owner: Ecuadorian Navy |
| Max height: 38.3m | Construction: Steel |
| Beam: 10.6m | Builder: ASTACE, Bilbao, Spain |
| Draught: 4.2m | Engine: 700 b.h.p., General Motors, diesel |

Photograph: Janka Bielak

# ALBANUS

The original *Albanus* was built in 1904 on a small island in the vast Aland archipelago, by one of the foremost master shipwrights J.A. Henrikson. During the nineteenth and early twentieth centuries, hundreds of similar galliasses plied the Baltic with their cargoes of fish, farm produce, firewood, etc. and laid the foundations for the great shipping tradition of the Aland Islands.

In 1988 the Cutty Sark Races made their first visit to Mariehamn, the capital of the Aland Islands, which reminded many of the more venerable locals of the past when the great Erikson fleet graced their harbour. The giant four-masted barque *Kruzenshtern* was moored in the same spot where she had been placed over fifty years before. During the visit, the replica *Albanus* was ceremonially launched.

Her building had been a two-year project and it all started when a society was formed to construct this ship. This provided the Islands with a fine symbol and gave their young people the benefits of sailing a traditional craft. By building *Albanus* the islands' conventional art of shipbuilding was also preserved and documented with the help of the fading generation of craftsmen.

Her traditional flax sails, which were hand sewn by old Cape Horn sailors, did nothing to slow her down in the 1992 Cutty Sark Race from Karlskrona to Kotka, where she was the first traditional craft to cross the finish line and was second overall on Corrected Time.

## DATA

| | |
|---|---|
| Year built: 1988 | Sail area: 300m² |
| Rig: Gaff ketch | Tonnage: 49 grt; 80 displacement; 19 net |
| Max length: 26.9m | Crew complement: 24 |
| Length of hull: 21.3m | Owner: Skepps Föreningen Albanus |
| Max height: 22.9m | Construction: Wood |
| Beam: 6.1m | Builder: J.A. Henrikson, Aland Islands, Finland |
| Draught: 2.0m | Engine: Volvo 220 b.h.p. diesel |

Photograph: Rita Jokiranta

# HELENA

This sleek staysail schooner was designed by a Frenchman, Guy Ribadeau Dumas. The traditional lines of her freeboard do not give away an almost modern fin and skeg shape that hide below her waterline and ensure that she performs well on all points of sailing.

Flagship of the Finnish Sail Training fleet, she made her début in the Baltic 1992 Cutty Sark Tall Ships' Races. That year the races visited Kotka and, headed by *Helena*, the Finnish fleet paraded themselves in force. This had been a remarkable achievement as they only had a very small fleet when the races first visited Finland in 1988. There is now an STA Finland which promotes and fulfils the same aims as the British STA.

Her build was completed in a very short time at the Uusikaupunki Shipyard in Finland, and it was a credit to Finnish craftsmanship that she went straight into operation with no problems. Financed by Finnish industry and commerce, the companies which have supported the project are able to host corporate events and invite guests out on day sails, and these subsidise the voyage fees the young Finnish crews need to pay.

*Helena* is one of the prettiest ships that participate in the races and, with her jackyard main topsail and great spread of canvas, she is probably one of the fastest schooners.

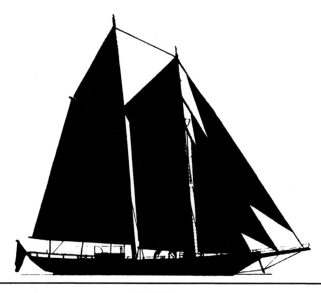

## DATA

| | |
|---|---|
| Year built: 1991 | Sail area: 532.2m² |
| Rig: 2-masted schooner | Tonnage: 98 displacement |
| Max length: 37.1m | Crew complement: 28 |
| Length of hull: 31.8m | Owner: STA Finland |
| Max height: 33.9m | Construction: Steel |
| Beam: 6.6m | Builder: Uusikaupunki Shipyard, Finland |
| Draught: 2.9m | Engine: 300 b.h.p., diesel |

Photograph: Suomen Purjelaivasäätiö

# BELLE POULE & ETOILE

The 'Goelettes de L'Ecole Navale' were constructed in 1932 at the French naval shipyard in Fécamp.
The identical sisters have been graced with the lines of a 'Paimpolaise schooner' which sailed
regularly to the coast of Newfoundland in search of cod during the late nineteenth century.
Their versatile rig now offers midshipmen of the French navy an opportunity to develop the finer
arts of seamanship, sailing and navigation. Based in Brest, the 'goelettes' carry sixteen permanent
crew and a total complement of thirty-one. Rarely seen apart, the beautiful sisters can often be
witnessed in harbour, staging a fine display of ship handling, and manoevering under power in
'catamaran' formation.
In the reign of King Loius XV, the pirate ship *Belle Poule* had rendered such service to the country it
was decreed that the name should be preserved in future ships of the French navy. The most
famous of the four vessels to bear this name was the ship which brought back Napoleon's exhumed
body to France in 1840. The name *L'Etoile* has been borne by fifteen French warships.

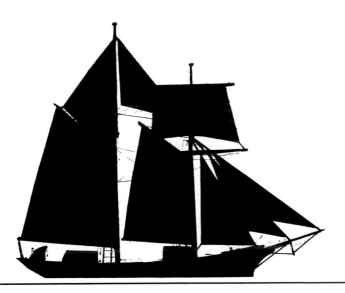

## DATA

| | |
|---|---|
| Year built: 1932 | Sail area: 553.2m² |
| Rig: Topsail schooner | Tonnage: 275 net |
| Max length: 37.2m | Crew complement: 31 |
| Length of hull: 30.4m | Owner: French Navy |
| Max height: 30.4m | Construction: Wood |
| Beam: 7.2m | Builder: Chantier Naval de Nomandie, Fécamp, France |
| Draught: 3.4m | Engine: 280 b.h.p. Bau Donin, diesel |

Photograph: Janka Bielak

# ALEXANDER VON HUMBOLDT

Designed as a lightship by the famous marine architect Frederick Middendorf, her sea-kindly, sailing ship hull proved ideally suited to the rigours of lightship duty in various parts of the Baltic and North Seas, where she was stationed for eighty years. Director of Germanic Lloyd at the time, Herr Middendorf had a fine reputation in ship design having already delivered the plans for the *Prussen*. This enormous five-masted barque was the greatest sailing vessel to have been constructed in all maritime history and carried the largest spread of canvas ever to have driven a windjammer. In 1986, the discerning eye of Captain Manfred Hovener recognised the potential of this lightship's perfectly formed hull. Inspired with the dream of providing a sailing ship for the youth of Germany, he set about the arduous task of searching for sponsors to finance a conversion to a three-masted barque. His success explains the striking green sails as Becks beer was the first major company to support this brave venture. He was also supported and given invaluable advice from the rich pool of experienced windjammer captains who were based around the Wesser.

On 30 March 1988 *Alex* began her rigorous sea trials and was certificated by Germanic Lloyd a couple of months later. Operated by STA Germany, she has fulfilled Captain Hovener's dream and has sailed many thousands of miles with countless young crews. A keen competitor in the Cutty Sark Tall Ships' Races, she can be easily identified by her bright green sails, and by her affectionately named 'hampster pouches', which are the gaps in the side of the ship where her crew stow all of those bits of equipment which never seem to have a place of their own.

## DATA

| | |
|---|---|
| Year built: 1906 | Sail area: 10,871.0m² |
| Rig: Barque | Tonnage: 396 grt; 829 displacement; 660 net |
| Max length: 62.6m | Crew complement: 60 |
| Length of hull: 54.1m | Owner: STA Germany |
| Max height: 31.6m | Construction: Steel |
| Beam: 8.1m | Builder: Weser, Bremen, Germany |
| Draught: 4.9m | Engine: 8 cyclinder, 510 b.h.p. Man, diesel |

Photograph: Janka Bielak

# GORCH FOCK II

Germany's commitment to training cadets under sail was tested to the full on 21 September 1957 when tragedy struck the four-masted barque *Pamir*. She was capsized by hurricane Carrie 600 miles south-west of the Azores and went down with the sad loss of eighty men, including fifty-two cadets.

At the same time *Gorch Fock II* was being constructed at the famous Blohm and Voss shipyard in Hamburg, but it was decided to continue her build and she was commissioned in 1958. Consequently, particular attention was given to testing her stability and seaworthiness and she underwent a thorough programme of sea trials.

Since her trials, she has been training cadets of the German navy and has earned herself a legendary reputation for smartness. Her cadets are always immaculately turned out and discipline is exemplary on board. She has four sisters *Tovarishch*, *Eagle*, *Sagres* and *Mircea*. All these training ships have the same beautifully shaped hull and are rigged similarly to three-masted barques. *Gorch Fock* can easily be distinguished by the golden-brown sides to her fo'c's'le and poop-deck, and by her beautifully carved figurehead of an albatross.

She is named after the famous maritime writer Johann Kinau, who used Gorch Fock as his nom de plume. He died in action during the First World War on a cruiser in the Skaggerak.

This fine barque and smart crew can often be seen during Cutty Sark Tall Ships' Races and she has an excellent race record to her credit.

## DATA

| | |
|---|---|
| Year built: 1958 | Sail area: 1,805.3m² |
| Rig: Barque | Tonnage: 1,499 grt; 1,727 tm |
| Max length: 88.2m | Crew complement: 269 |
| Length of hull: 81.0m | Owner: German Navy |
| Max height: 45.1m | Construction: Steel |
| Beam: 11.9m | Builder: Blohm & Voss Shipyard, Hamburg, Germany |
| Draught: 5.3m | Engine: 800 b.h.p. Man, diesel |

Photograph: Janka Bielak

# GROSSHERZOGIN ELIZABETH

In 1983 this three-masted schooner received her fifth name when she was bought by the Elsfleth Nautical College of Germany. She started her life in 1909 as *San Antonio* when she was built in the Netherlands as an auxiliary trading schooner, and spent the next three decades plying the African coast. In 1940 her rig was removed and a more powerful diesel engine was installed.

In 1947 she was sold to a Swedish owner and renamed *Buddi* and she continued to trade in the Baltic and North Sea. During several further changes of ownership she received the name of *Santoni* returning to her original name of *San Antonio*. She eventually was given her sailing rig back in 1973 when she converted to a charter vessel. She also received a large deckhouse during the process which, although it provides the charterers with an extra degree of comfort, does make her less graceful. She is used extensively as a charter ship in the Caribbean and Mediterranean as well as the Baltic.

She often participates in the Cutty Sark Races, particularly the Baltic and North Sea series. She is distinguishable by her long deckhouse which is almost unbroken between her fo'c's'le and poop deck, and has only one yard which is unusual for a ship of this size.

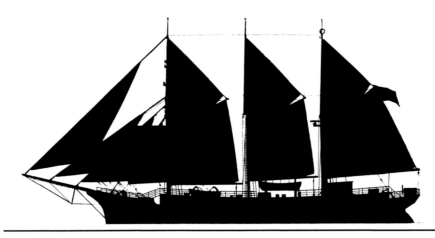

## DATA

| | |
|---|---|
| Year built: 1909 | Sail area: 1,010m² |
| Rig: 3-masted schooner | Tonnage: 462 grt |
| Max length: 64.4m | Crew complement: 51 |
| Length of hull: 53.1m | Owner: Schulschiffverein Grossherzogin |
| Max height: 33.0m | Construction: Iron |
| Beam: 8.2m | Builder: Scheepswerven Jan Smidt, Alblasserdam, Netherlands |
| Draught: 2.5m | Engine: 400 b.h.p. Caterpillar, diesel |

Photograph: Janka Bielak

# JOHANN SMIDT

Originally built as *Eendracht*, this two-masted topsail schooner was bought in 1989 by the Clipper Deutsches Jugendworkz See which also own *Seute Deern, Albatros* and *Amphitrite*. However, this change in ownership has not stopped her from voyaging to the warmer weather in the winter as she did with her previous owners, as the Clipper Foundation also operate her in the Canary Islands biennially between November and March.

With a new home port of Bremen, she generally cruises within the Baltic and North Sea taking young members of the foundation to sea between the ages of sixteen and twenty-seven. Her captain and experienced crew are all volunteers and do not get paid for their professional services, which helps to keep the running costs relatively low. This is the same way that *Alexander von Humboldt* is operated and affirms the enthusiasm and dedication of sail training in Germany.

A keen supporter of the Cutty Sark Tall Ships' Races, this schooner is surprisingly fast and has many trophies to her name.

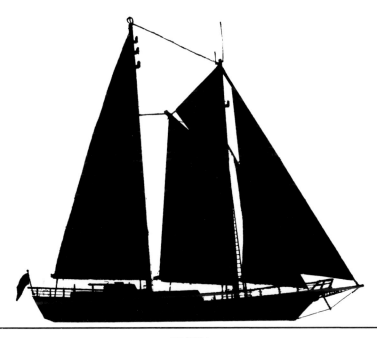

## DATA

| | |
|---|---|
| Year built: 1974 | Sail area: 527.6m² |
| Rig: Schooner | Tonnage: 226 tm |
| Max length: 35.6m | Crew complement: 38 |
| Length of hull: 32.6m | Owner: German Clipper Society |
| Max height: 33.8m | Construction: Steel |
| Beam: 7.9m | Builder: Commenga, Amsterdam, Netherlands |
| Draught: 3.6m | Engine: 400 b.h.p., General Motors, diesel |

Photograph: Janka Bielak

# ASGARD II

This beautiful brigantine was designed and built in Arklow by the late Jack Tyrell and commissioned in 1981. *Asgard* is an old Norse word meaning 'Home of the Gods' and was given to the Colin Archer designed ketch, which was the first vessel to take young people from Ireland sail training. However, the original *Asgard* once carried a very different cargo when in 1914 she transported a shipment of guns from Hamburg to Howth in Ireland. The owner and famous author of The Riddle of the Sands was later executed for his part in this and the ketch was eventually purchased by the Coiste An Asgard, the current operators of *Asgard II*.

Every year from early spring to late autumn she carries out one- to three-week cruise programmes; unless she is participating in a Cutty Sark Tall Ships' Race which is often longer. Occasionally she will sail out of European and Baltic waters, as in 1985 when she visited the United States. In 1988 she basically completed a circumnavigation when she participated in the Australian bicentennial celebrations, but this time it was in a less dignified way as the brigantine was deck cargo on a large container ship. The ship, her young crew and her huge tricolour ensign proved to be great ambassadors for their country and impressed the Irish Community 'down under'.

Her win of the coveted Cutty Sark Trophy in 1991 was particularly appropriate, as this was the first year the fleet had raced to Ireland.

## DATA

| | |
|---|---|
| Year built: 1981 | Sail area: 388.9m² |
| Rig: Brigantine | Tonnage: 93 grt |
| Max length: 31.0m | Crew complement: 25 |
| Length of hull: 26.6m | Owner: Coiste An Asgard |
| Max height: 33.5m | Construction: Wood |
| Beam: 6.4m | Builder: Tyrell & Sons, Arklow, Rep of Ireland |
| Draught: 2.9m | Engine: 160 b.h.p. diese! |

Photograph: Janka Bielak

# AMERIGO VESPUCCI

This easily-recognised ship was designed along the lines of a nineteenth-century, three-decked line of battle ship. She was one of a pair built in 1928 and 1931, but her elder sister *Christoforo Columbo* was taken as a war prize by the Russians and was renamed *Danuy* (Danube). Mussolini decreed that these ships were to be built and, although *Amerigo Vespucci* is as immaculate as she was on the day she was launched, her sister was sadly broken up in Odessa in 1971. Both ships were named after famous explorers and *Amerigo Vespucci* of course proudly bears the name of the fifteenth-century Florentine merchant and adventurer (1451–1512).

She is one of the most impressive sailing ships afloat today and always attracts considerable attention whilst in port, with her gilded stern with gallery, her striking black and white hull and her towering narrow rig. Her trainees are as polished as her brass work and usually spend three months aboard this spectacular vessel, training in the Mediterranean and Atlantic for a career in the Italian navy.

She occasionally joins in the Cutty Sark fleet celebrations, but never races as her traditional nineteenth-century design means she has a nineteenth-century performance.

## DATA

Year built: 1931          Sail area: 3,469.7m²
Rig: Full-rigged ship     Tonnage: 2,686 tm; 4,100 displacement
Max length: 123.5m        Crew complement: 409
Length of hull: 100.5m    Owner: Italian Navy
Max height: 62.1m         Construction: Steel
Beam: 13.9m               Builder: Castellamare di Stabia Shipyard, Naples, Italy
Draught: 8.7m             Engine: 2 x 950 b.h.p. Fiat, diesel

Photograph: Janka Bielak

# KAISEI

Originally named *Zew* and built as a topsail schooner at Gdansk, Poland in 1990, this beautifully proportioned vessel was a victim of the Polish economic problems and was subsequently sold in Antigua to the Japanese Sail Training Association. Afterwards, she was sailed back to Poland for a basic refit, and inspected by the Japanese Ministry of Transport. She completed her conversion into a brigantine in the 'sail training friendly' port of Weymouth during 1991. This final stage of her refit was carried out largely with the help of dedicated volunteers from many countries.
Later that year she set sail for the Mediterranean, eventually joining up with the Grand Regatta Columbus fleet at Cadiz in April 1992. The only Japanese entrant in this historical event, she also flew the United Nations flag and continued with the international fleet to New York, where she turned south for the Panama canal and onwards to Japan where she is based today.
The brainchild of the famous Japanese ocean racing yachtsman Kaoru Ogimi, *Kaisei* has already contributed a great deal to the international world of sail training.

## DATA

Year built: 1988
Rig: Brigantine
Max length: 43.3m
Length of hull: 35.3m
Max height: 32.0m
Beam: 7.5m
Draught: 4.0m

Sail area: 780m²
Tonnage: 180 grt; 54 net
Crew complement: 45
Owner: STA Japan
Construction: Steel
Builder: Gdansk Shipyard, Poland
Engine: 200 b.h.p. diesel

Photograph: Cutty Sark Scots Whisky

# KAIWO MARU & NIPPON MARU

Although both these mighty sisters appear to be traditional square-riggers, they were in fact built during the 1980s to replace their predecessors of the same names. Considerable wind tunnel testing and computer-generated projections went into developing these ships, and consequently advances in safety, strength and performance have been achieved. These are probably the most technologically advanced sailing ships in the world. However, they only really differ visually from their predecessors by their unbroken decks, double spankers and lack of funnel for their auxiliary engines.

Most Japanese merchant ships are suffixed with 'maru' which broadly translates to 'endeavour'. 'Kaiwo' means 'king of the sea' and Nippon is of course Japan. Built by the Japanese steel giant Sumitomo Heavy Industries Ltd they were the first large sailing vessels to be built in Japan for over half a century, and were commissioned by the Institute for Sea Training of the Ministry of Transport. By the time *Kaiwo Maru* was launched in 1989 she had cost an estimated £45 million which gives some indication of what a full-sized sail training ship would cost today.

Both sisters have represented their country in international events such as the 1988 Australian bicentennial celebrations and the 1992 Columbus Regatta. The previous *Nippon Maru* is now a tourist attraction in the port of Yokohama.

## DATA

Year built: 1989
Rig: 4-masted barque
Max length: 110.1m
Length of hull: 95.0m
Max height: 55.5m
Beam: 13.8m
Draught: 6.6m

Sail area: 2,760m²
Tonnage: 2,879 grt; 4,655 displacement; 1,425 net
Crew complement: 199
Owner: Ministry of Transport, Japan
Construction: Steel
Builder: Unaga Dockyard, Sumitomo Heavy Industries Ltd, Japan
Engine: 2 x 1,500 b.h.p. Daihatsu, diesel

Photograph: Janka Bielak

# TUNAS SAMUDERA

*Young Endeavour* has a sistership named *Tunas Samudera*, which means 'offspring of the ocean' in Malaysian. She was built in 1989 and presented to the Royal Malaysian Navy by H.M. the Queen on 16 October 1989. It has been suggested that she was given to the Malaysians as part of a contract to buy British naval equipment. She is virtually identical to her Australian sister, but *Tunas Samudera* has a white hull instead of 'Britannia blue'.

She was designed by Colin Mudie who also created *Lord Nelson* and *Royalist*. Like her Australian sister she makes an ideal two-masted training ship, there has been considerable thought to the accommodation layout below and her rig and deck plan is excellent. Her distinctive lines are Victorian in style, and her architect believes that she might start a trend in sail training ship aesthetics in the future.

Her main operational objective is to provide Malaysian youth with an adventure under sail whilst cultivating their personal and leadership skills. She generally operates twenty ten-day voyages throughout the year, and the young crew learn the arts of seamanship, navigation, meteorology, oceanography and ship husbandry.

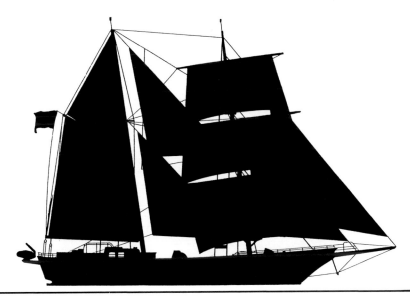

## DATA

| | |
|---|---|
| Year built: 1987 | Sail area: 649.1m² |
| Rig: Brigantine | Tonnage: 239 displacement; 175 grt |
| Max length: 42.1m | Crew complement: 37 |
| Length of hull: 34.9m | Owner: Royal Malaysian Navy |
| Max height: 30.7m | Construction: Steel |
| Beam: 7.9m | Builder: Brooke Yachts, Lowestoft, UK |
| Draught: 3.7m | Engine: 2 x Perkins V8 185 b.h.p. diesel |

Photograph: Colin Mudie

# EENDRACHT

This 60-metre schooner was commissioned to replace her smaller predecessor, *Johann Smidt*, because of the growing enthusiasm in the Netherlands for young people 'to go before the mast' and to represent this seagoing nation throughout the world. A modern and sumptuous design was decided upon so that she could operate as a charter vessel.

The keel was laid in September 1988 by H.R.H. Prince Bernard and she was graciously named by H.M. Queen Beatrix on 29 August 1989. It was a remarkable feat to have built this fine ship to such a high standard in so short a time and exemplifies the excellence of Dutch sailing ship and yacht building. Funded by business and private contributions, it cost £2.7 million.

*Eendracht* now operates for 330 days a year and winters in the Canary Islands in order to subsidise her youth training programme during the summer. With a modern hull and keel design she is very fast, and this was proved when she attained a speed of 15 knots in a Beaufort wind force 5 during the Cutty Sark Tall Ships' Race from Plymouth to La Coruña in 1990.

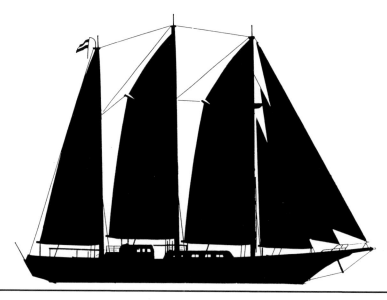

## DATA

Year built: 1989  
Rig: Schooner  
Max length: 58.8m  
Length of hull: 55.3m  
Max height: 41.6m  
Beam: 12.3m  
Draught: 5.0m  

Sail area: 1,047m²  
Tonnage: 600 displacement  
Crew complement: 53  
Operator: Het Zeilend Zeeschip, Scheveningen  
Construction: Steel  
Builder: Damen Shipyard, Gorinchem, Netherlands  
Engine: 540 b.h.p. Caterpillar, diesel  

Photograph: Cutty Sark Scots Whisky

# URANIA

Pride of the Dutch navy, this beautiful ketch has an outstanding record for training their midshipmen. The style of discipline aboard is relaxed and friendly, but there is a high level of professionalism throughout the crew. This is easier to achieve and is more usual aboard the smaller vessels. Twice winner of the coveted Cutty Sark Trophy she has always been a favourite amongst the competing crews.

Built over sixty years ago as only the Dutch know how to build steel yachts, she is always maintained to a high standard. With her powerful rig and large sail area, she can be driven along at good speed in heavy weather. She has excellent sea-keeping qualities for a relatively small vessel. However, in the 1984 race from Bermuda to Halifax when tragedy struck the *Marques*, she too was almost lost when a large sea tore off a large hatch in her cockpit. The breaking seas threatened to overwhelm her as her pumps were not coping with the down flooding. The race guard-ship, the Canadian frigate *Assinaboine*, arrived just in time and put on board a large pump which saved the day.

She continues to participate in most Cutty Sark Races and operates a full training programme around Europe and Scandinavia.

## DATA

| | |
|---|---|
| Year built: 1928 | Sail area: 293.5m² |
| Rig: Bermudan ketch | Tonnage: 65 displacement |
| Max length: 21.9m | Crew complement: 18 |
| Length of hull: 21.9m | Owner: Royal Netherlands Navy |
| Max height: 26.17m | Construction; Steel |
| Beam: 5.2m | Builder: Haarlemsche Scheepsbouw Maatschappij, |
| Draught: 2.8m | Netherlands |

Photograph: Janka Bielak

# CHRISTIAN RADICH

During the 1970s this beautifully proportioned, full-rigged ship starred in the television series The Onedin Line as a cargo carrying vessel. Ironically she has never carried cargo as she was designed by Captain Blohm with sail training in mind for the Christiania School Ship Association.
The Oslo based association (Christiania being the original name of Oslo) first started training with the British barque *Lady Grey* in 1877 and later the brig *Statsraad Erickson* with the full-rigged ship *Mersy*. It was intended to rename *Mersy* to *Christian Radich* after the Norwegian businessman (of Danish origin) who had bequeathed 50,000 krone to build a training ship; but she was sold due to the outbreak of the First World War.
Her keel was laid in 1935 at the Framnaes Mek-Verksted yard in Sandefjord and two years later she replaced her aging predecessor *Statsraad Erickson*. After completing her return passage from the New York World Fair in 1940 she was seized by the Germans in Horten Naval Base in Oslo Fjord during the invasion of Norway. Her temporary demise during the war began when she was used as a submarine depot ship, and in 1943 she was towed to Germany after the association refused to use her to train their naval cadets. After the war she was found capsized in a sad state at Flensburg, but with help of the Allies she was righted and returned to her builders for a major rebuild.
In 1949 she resumed her training programme and the Christiania School Ship Association was renamed the Ostlandets Skoeskib who still remain the owners. She was second in the first race from Torbay to Lisbon in 1956, and first in some other major races including the 1992 Columbus Regatta, where she emerged first on Corrected Time against a large competitive fleet which raced from Cadiz to Puerto Rico.
She now benefits from a larger auxiliary engine which was fitted in 1963 and a modernized accommodation plan which was completed during her 1983 major refit. To supplement the cadets' training and with decreasing opportunities to make a career in the Norwegian fighting or merchantile navies, she operates some passenger cruises in warmer climates from time to time.

## DATA

| | |
|---|---|
| Year built: 1937 | Sail area: 1,387.5m² |
| Rig: Full-rigged ship | Tonnage: 676 grt |
| Max length: 72.1m | Crew complement: 104 |
| Length of hull: 62.8m | Owner: Ostlandets Skoeskib, Oslo, Norway |
| Max height: 36.1m | Construction: Steel |
| Beam: 9.7m | Builder: Framnaes Mek-Verksted A/S, Sandefjord, Norway |
| Draught: 4.6m | Engine: 450 b.h.p. General Motors, diesel |

Photograph: Cutty Sark Scots Whisky

# COLIN ARCHER

The most famous double-ended sailing vessel of all time, *Colin Archer* is named after the gifted man who designed her. Her successful design was a result of a competition which was staged in the hope of finding a suitable rescue boat to protect the Norwegian fishing fleet whilst working off their inhospitable and rugged coastline. These rescue boats needed to be extremely strong, seaworthy, fast, easily handled and able to be sailed off a leeshore in any conditions. Colin Archer's design was found to have all these qualities and consequently this was the first vessel of many in its class to be built.

In later years the design was modified to take an auxiliary engine and the ships continued to save many Norwegian fishermen's lives over the decades.

*Colin Archer* has been restored and is a working example of Norway's history and tradition. She is based in Colin Archer's home town of Larvik, which is a picturesque settlement situated in the Oslo Fjord. She is also dedicated to training young Norwegians and is a regular participant in the Cutty Sark Tall Ships' Races.

This class of vessel has stretched the STA Rule of Rating, as she appears to defy the fundamental rules of hydro-dynamics. There is no doubt that Colin Archer's design was well ahead of its time, but her peformance never ceases to amaze competing captains – she has been known to beat modern yachts like Nicholson 55's on actual time!

## DATA

| | |
|---|---|
| Year built: 1893 | Sail area: 114.3m² |
| Rig: Gaff-rigged ketch | Tonnage: 27 displacement |
| Max length: 17.7m | Crew complement: 7 |
| Length of hull: 13.9m | Construction: Wood |
| Max height: 17.91m | Builder: Tolderodden, Norway |
| Beam: 4.7m | |
| Draught: 2.1m | |

Photograph: Janka Bielak

# STATSRAAD LEHMKUHL

Originally named *Grossherzog Friederich August*, this majestic three-masted barque was built as a training ship for the German Merchant Marine in 1914 by Johann C. Tecklenborg AG, Bremerhaven. During the Great War, although she was used for training, she hardly went to sea, and in 1918 she was taken by the British as a war prize.

In 1922 the Director of Bergen, and former minister, inspired the Norwegian Shipowners' Association to buy her for 300,000 Norwegian krone. In appreciation of this and for his work in the 1905 Cabinet, the ship was renamed *Statsraad Lehmkuhl* (Minister Lehmkuhl). She was transferred to the Bergen School Ship Foundation in 1923 after completing a successful training voyage with about 200 trainees. In 1940, she was confiscated by Germany and renamed *Westwarts* but was returned at the end of the war and continued with the school until 1966. During her latter time with the school she visited New York in 1952 and in 1964 as part of the Tall Ships' fleet which had raced from Lisbon via Bermuda.

Having enjoyed financial support from the Norwegian government for a while, this was withdrawn in 1967, but she was saved by the Bergen shipowner Hilmar Reksten who bought and started to refit her. She remained alongside in her berth for many years but finally set sail again with a programme of training and commercial charter. She was one of the stars of The Onedin Line in the 1970s and has since accompanied the Cutty Sark Tall Ships' fleet in some European and Scandinavian ports.

## DATA

Year built: 1914
Rig: 3-masted barque
Max length: 84.21m
Length of hull: 70.5m
Beam: 12.65m
Draught: 5.21m

Tonnage: 2,012 tm
Crew complement: 180
Construction: Steel
Builder: J.C. Tecklenborg, Bremerhaven, Germany
Engine: 450 b.h.p. diesel

Photograph: Cutty Sark Scots Whisky

# SHABAB OMAN

This impressive barquentine started life as the three-masted topsail schooner *Captain Scott* operating Outward Bound courses off the rugged north-west coast of Scotland. She was built in 1971 for the Dulverton Trust by the famous fishing boat builders Herd and Mackenzie of Buckie. Her original permanent crew of seven included John Hamilton (STA Race Director 1976–1992) and John Fisher (captain of *Lord Nelson*). Her Outward Bound voyages lasted for twenty-five days each, during which her trainees would be dropped off at various isolated spots to take part in hill and mountain expeditions. They would also undergo a programme of training at sea, learning the art of seamanship as well as the importance of working in a team. This challenging combination is an ideal way of training young people to be resourceful, adaptable and capable of handling demanding situations.

The principal designer of the largest wooden sail training ship in commission today was the late Robert Clark who was better known for his ability to create beautiful yachts. Amongst the many he designed are the Ocean Youth Club 72-foot ketches which are still doing sterling service as sail training vessels today. Her original captain (the late Victor Scott) and Captain Willoughby were also involved in the design of this fine ship.

Regrettably she was laid up in 1975 when it was realised that her optimistic programme of long voyages was not financially viable without assistance from the government, and she was eventually sold to the Sultan of Oman in 1977. She was renamed *Youth of Oman* and handed over to the Ministry of Youth Affairs to operate. She was repainted white so that the heat of the sun would be reflected and protect her wooden hull. Two years later she was transferred to the Omani navy and her name translated into Arabic, and in 1984 she was converted to a barquentine.

This is a sail training ship which is used to the full, not only operating around the Arabian Sea but flying the flag for her country all over the world. She has participated in the large gatherings such as the Australian bicentennial celebrations in 1988 and the Columbus Regatta in 1992 as well as some fairly recent Cutty Sark Tall Ships' Races. She is easily identified under sail as her topsails are adorned with the red dagger and crossed swords which is Oman's national symbol.

## DATA

Year built: 1971
Rig: Barquentine
Max length: 51.5m
Length of hull: 43.9m
Max height: 32.0m
Beam: 8.5m
Draught: 4.7m

Sail area: 835m²
Tonnage: 264 grt; 490 displacement; 55 net
Crew complement: 58
Owner: Omani Navy
Construction: Wood
Builder: Herd & Mackenzie, Buckie, Scotland
Engine: 2 x 250 b.h.p. Caterpillar, diesel

Photograph: Janka Bielak

# DAR MLODZIEZY

*Dar Mlodziezy*, 'gift of youth' in Polish, was commissioned to replace the famous *Dar Pomorza* (gift of the Polish Sea States), which for fifty years trained officers of the Polish merchant navy. Designed by a Polish team, which was headed by Mr Zygmant Choren, the B-95 type was a development from the very successful smaller *Pogoria* class barquentine.

Launched in 1982, she made her début in the Cutty Sark Tall Ships' Race from Falmouth to Lisbon, Vigo and Southampton. Since then she has been a keen supporter of the races, competing in the 1984 transatlantic race to Quebec and the 1986 North Sea series. During these events she has won numerous prizes and has taken line honours in her class on many occasions. In 1988 she set off on her first circumnavigation, and stole the show at the Australian bicentennial celebrations when she passed under the Sydney Harbour Bridge with all sails set! This was quite a feat, as she had only a clearance of one metre. She returned safely the following year, having experienced some severe weather off Cape Horn, and since then has continued to train merchant naval officers in the Baltic, European and American waters.

To underline the success of this design, *Dar Mlodziezy* now has five sister ships which are operated by Russia: *Khersones, Mir, Pallada, Druzhba* and *Nadezhda*. These have all been constructed at the shipyard in Gdansk, with only slight modifications to the sail plan and deck structure.

## DATA

| | |
|---|---|
| Year built: 1982 | Sail area: 3,137.5m² |
| Rig: Full-rigged ship | Tonnage: 2, 385 grt |
| Max length: 109.2m | Crew complement: 194 |
| Length of hull: 94.2m | Owner: Merchant Marine Academy, Gdynia, Poland |
| Max height: 50.1m | Construction: Steel |
| Beam: 13.9m | Builder: Gdansk Shipyard, Poland |
| Draught: 6.3m | Engine: 2 x 750 b.h.p., Cegielski-Sulzer, diesel |

Photograph: Cutty Sark Scots Whisky

# FRYDERYK CHOPIN

Named after the great nineteenth-century maestro, *Fryderyk Chopin* is probably the fastest brig ever to be launched and was designed by the famous Zygmunt Choren. Choren was able to assimilate data which he had gained by designing the *Dar Mlodziezy* and *Pogoria* classes. During the first year this state-of-the-art square-rigger entered the Columbus Regatta and gained a credible fifth place overall on Corrected Time out of almost one hundred vessels. Her unusually long bowsprit enables her to set six headsails, which together with her lofty masts means that she can take advantage of light winds. Although she is proportionately beamier than the other Choren designs, the shape of her bow is very similar. Her stern is quite distinctive however, with the main mast being positioned a long way forward.

Operated by the International Class Afloat Foundation, *Fryderyk Chopin* principally takes sixteen-year-old youngsters who attend conventional lessons in addition to undertaking the usual duties of a crew member. This is an excellent form of education and one which should be considered seriously by more education authorities. One of the key persons who was instrumental in the conception of this project is the famous Polish single-handed sailor Krzysztof Baranowski who bravely circumnavigated the globe in 1972/3 in the yacht *Polonez*.

## DATA

| | |
|---|---|
| Year built: 1990 | Sail area: 1,345.5m² |
| Rig: Brig | Tonnage: 306 grt; 400 displacement |
| Max length: 54.1m | Crew complement: 56 |
| Length of hull: 43.8m | Operator: International Class Afloat |
| Max height: 36.22m | Construction: Steel |
| Beam: 8.5m | Builder: Gdansk Shipyard, Poland |
| Draught: 3.8m | Engine: 2 x 240 b.h.p. Wola, hydraulic propulsion, diesel |

Photograph: Cutty Sark Scots Whisky

# HENRYK RUTKOWSKI

There are many vessels that have been converted to sail but *Henryk Rutkowski* has been one of the most successful. With her well-proportioned brigantine rig, she makes a fine little sail training ship. Originally built in 1944 as a German navy patrol cutter, her lines were based on an earlier Dutch pilot schooner which was noted for its sailing qualities. In fact pilot cutters throughout Europe were renowned for being seaworthy and able sailing craft, as they needed to be at sea in all weathers and fast to catch the business. She is appropriately named after a Polish resistance fighter as she was seized by the Poles at the end of the Second World War.

Her first voyage as a sailing ship was in 1951 as a gaff ketch when she began to train Polish fishermen. That stage of her career ended in 1976 when she was decommissioned as she was in need of a major refit, but the necessary finance did not become available until 1984. After a successful refit, she was recommissioned in 1986. During that two-year period the wooden main deck was replaced with a steel one and her rig converted to a brigantine. Her after-deck was raised to create more room for accommodation below and to provide an excellent position from which to command the ship.

Her début Cutty Sark Race was in 1989 when she arrived in the Pool of London and continued on to Hamburg. Her captain and crew were quick to integrate well within the fleet and she earned a reputation as one of the most popular ships. She is surprisingly fast and there is usually friendly rivalry between her, *Royalist* and *Asgard*.

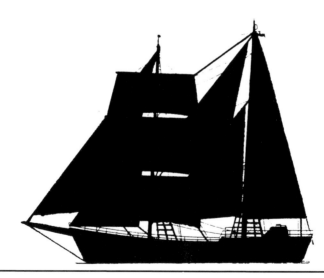

## DATA

Year built: 1944
Rig: Brigantine
Max length: 28.42m
Length of hull: 24.02m
Max height: 22.45m
Beam: 6.46m
Draught: 3.22m

Sail area: 349.5m²
Tonnage: 99.43 grt
Crew complement: 25
Owner: Centralny Osrobek Zeglarstwa, Trzebiez, Poland
Construction: Wood/steel
Builder: Swinemünde, Germany
Engine: 121 b.h.p. diesel

Photograph: Cutty Sark Scots Whisky

# ORP ISKRA

The second *Iskra* came into service on 11 August 1982, replacing the original three-masted schooner which had served the Polish navy from 1927 until 1977. As she is a ship of the Polish navy her name is usually prefixed by ORP.
This sleek barquentine was designed by the famous Polish naval architect Zygmant Choren (see *Dar Mlodziezy*) and built in Gdansk at the Lenin Shipyard, which has now been renamed after the Solidarity uprising of 1981 which started there. The first of this successful class was *Pogoria*, and *ORP Iskra*, the second to be built, mainly differs by her hull shape around the stern which has been hydro-dynamically improved. Her deck layout is also different from her sisters *Pogoria, Kaliakra* and *Oceania* as they have all been customised to their individual needs.
Training young cadets from the Westerplatte Heroes Naval Academy for a future in the Polish navy is *ORP Iskra*'s role, and therefore she has been furnished with some state-of-the-art navigational equipment like an electronic chart system which enables her position to be plotted on a video screen anywhere in the world.
*ORP Iskra* has completed two double transatlantic crossings and is a loyal supporter of the Cutty Sark Tall Ships' Races, winning the much-coveted Cutty Sark Trophy in 1989.

## DATA

| | |
|---|---|
| Year built: 1982 | Sail area: 954.4m² |
| Rig: Barquentine | Tonnage: 289 grt |
| Max length: 48.4m | Crew complement: 67 |
| Length of hull: 42.7m | Owner: Polish Navy |
| Max height: 33.5m | Construction: Steel |
| Beam: 8.0m | Builder: Gdansk Shipyard, Poland |
| Draught: 3.2m | Engine: 310 b.h.p. diesel |

Photograph: Cutty Sark Scots Whisky

# ZAWISZA CZARNY

This three-masted staysail schooner is certainly not one of the fastest ships in the fleet but it usually carries the most musical crew which is made up of Polish Pathfinder Sea Scouts. One of their primary missions is to preserve the maritime arts, especially maritime music and dance. They can often be seen in port during a race series bringing their traditional arts to life, performing sea shanties with a blend of mid-European choral folk harmonies and dance rhythms.

The first *Zawisza Czarny* was bought by the Polish Scouts' Union (ZHP) in 1934. This Swedish wooden schooner was originally built in 1901 under the name of *Petrea*. In 1965/6 the Polish Scouts' Union converted the 1952 fishing vessel *Cietrzew* into the sailing ship she is today, although she also received another major refit in 1980. She also received the name of *Zawisza Czarny* which came from the famous fifteenth-century Polish knight who was the hero of the battle of Grunwald in 1410. This venerable knight was renowned for keeping his word, and the well-known saying 'as reliable as Zawisza' is still used today in Poland.

This sturdy ship has entered many Cutty Sark Races as well as operating her usual fortnightly training voyages in the Baltic for nominated members of the Polish Sea Scout movement. In 1984 she bravely saved many lives when the *Marques* went down off Bermuda in severe local conditions. Her crew returned to Bermuda as heroes, after being on station for some considerable time searching for survivors in heavy seas and appalling conditions.

In 1992 she entered the Columbus Regatta completing all but the last leg of the race series, when she undertook an expedition off the Labrador Coast, before returning to Liverpool.

## DATA

| | |
|---|---|
| Year built: 1952 | Sail area: 618.2m² |
| Rig: Staysail schooner | Tonnage: 171 net |
| Max length: 42.7m | Crew complement: 46 |
| Length of hull: 36.1m | Owner: Polish Scouts |
| Beam: 6.7m | Construction: Steel |
| Draught: 4.5m | Engine: 390 b.h.p. diesel |

Photograph: Janka Bielak

# BOA ESPERANCA

This near-replica Portuguese caravelle was commissioned because of the success of her elder sister, *Bartholomeu Dias*. This vessel re-enacted the historical voyage from Portugal around the Cape of Good Hope in 1488, by the famous Portuguese navigator and explorer after whom she was named. *Bartholomeu Dias* is now a museum ship in Mossel Bay, but *Boa Esperanca* is actively taking the youth of Portugal on sail training voyages and is operated by Aporvela (STA Portugal).

Although the philosophy was to build her authentically, as it was with her sister, and the general appearance is similar, allowances were made to create a vessel which would be able to fulfil the objectives of sail training. For example, she has an engine, a refrigerator and modern electronic navigational equipment which those ancient navigators could never have imagined.

In her first few years she has proved herself to be a seaworthy and successful craft visiting northern Europe in 1990 and participating in the transatlantic Columbus Regatta in 1992. Her punishing schedule continues well into the future with a possible voyage to the Cape Verde Islands and South America, as well as attending the occasional Cutty Sark gathering.

## DATA

| | |
|---|---|
| Year built: 1990 | Sail area: 239.3m² |
| Rig: Caravelle | Crew complement: 22 |
| Max length: 24.3m | Owner: Aporvela, Portugal |
| Length of hull: 24.3m | Construction: Wood |
| Max height: 26.17m | |
| Beam: 6.5m | |
| Draught: 3.2m | |

Photograph: Janka Bielak

# CREOULA

Today, six officers, thirty-four permanent crew and fifty-two cadets have replaced the original cargo of 800 tons of salted fish and 60 tons of cod liver oil on board this Grand Banks schooner. No longer does she brave the icy fishing grounds of Greenland and Newfoundland but she stays in the warmer climes around Portugal and in the Mediterranean, offering the Portuguese youth of today an opportunity of experiencing the adventure of sail training.

Launched in March 1937, she was delivered to her original owners, Parceria Geral De Pescarias, the following May. By 1976 she had completed thirty-seven fishing expeditions before the conversion was started to make her into the handsome sail training ship that she is today. In 1987 she was completed and handed over to the Ministry of National Defence where she was designated an Auxiliary Naval Unit (VAM 201).

Operated by the Portuguese sister organisation to the Sail Training Association and with the assistance of the Portuguese navy, *Creoula* and her naval crew take civilian youngsters and naval cadets alike and she sometimes ventures north in order to participate in the Cutty Sark Tall Ships' Races. Her unusual four-masted schooner rig is particularly suited to strong reaching conditions and in the races held under these conditions she has been known to attain speeds in excess of 14 knots.

## DATA

| | |
|---|---|
| Year built: 1937 | Sail area: 1,545.5m² |
| Rig: 4-masted schooner | Tonnage: 676 displacement |
| Max length: 67.1m | Crew complement: 92 |
| Length of hull: 62.2m | Owner: Aporvela, Portugal |
| Max height: 36.8m | Construction: Steel/wood |
| Beam: 9.9m | |
| Draught: 5.6m | |

Photograph: Barry Pickthall/PPI

# SAGRES II

This beautiful, three-masted white barque is easily identified under sail from her Blohm and Voss sisters (*Tovarishch, Eagle, Mircea II,* and *Gorch Fock II*) by her red Maltese Crosses which adorn her square sails.

Built in 1937, she was named after the Portuguese naval town of Sagres near Cape St Vincent, where Prince Henry the Navigator established Europe's first navigation school and where he mounted his explorations and studied during the first half of the fifteenth century. She has the famous Portuguese navigator as her figurehead.

Her predecessor was also built in Germany as *Rickmer Rickmers* in Bremerhaven by the Richmers family and, having been renamed *Marx, Flores, Sagres I,* and *Santo Andro,* returned to her original name as a museum ship in Hamburg where she is to this day.

Her Blohm and Voss replacement, *Albert Leo Schlageter,* was handed over to the Portuguese in 1961 having been used by the Brazilian navy for training their cadets, under the name of *Guarnabara.*

Launched in 1937, she had a lucky escape during the Second World War when she struck a mine and was laid up until the United States took her as a 'windfall prize', eventually handing her over to the Brazilians two years later. She competed in the 1984 Tall Ships' Race from Bermuda to Halifax, Gaspe, Quebec, Cape Breton Island and Liverpool. She lost to her sisters *Gorch Fock* and *Eagle.* She also competed in the Columbus Regatta.

## DATA

| | |
|---|---|
| Year built: 1937 | Sail area: 1,896.5m² |
| Rig: Barque | Tonnage: 1,727 tm |
| Max length: 88.9m | Crew complement: 243 |
| Length of hull: 81.6m | Owner: Portuguese Navy |
| Max height: 45.1m | Construction: Steel |
| Beam: 12.1m | Builder: Blohm & Voss, Hamburg, Germany |
| Draught: 5.2m | Engine: 750 b.h.p. Man, diesel |

Photograph: Janka Bielak

# KRUZENSHTERN

Launched as *Padua* for the Flying P Line on 24 June 1926, when steam had largely taken over from sail in the merchant navies of the world. Although basically designed for cargo carrying, she had a complement of forty boys under instruction in all aspects of pratical seamanship, and started life plying between Europe and South America in the nitrate trade.

When rounding Cape Horn in 1830, tragedy struck and she lost four men in severe weather. However, she made many fast passages during a most successful career and later, when moved to the Australian grain trade, she took sixty-seven days to reach Port Lincoln from Hamburg. Her fastest noon to noon run was reputed to be 351 nautical miles on 28 December 1933.

In 1946 she was taken over by the USSR and renamed after the famous Russian navigator and hydrographer, Admiral Ivan Kruzenshtern. Since then she has trained many thousands of cadets for a career in the Fishery Board and in 1974 made history when she was the first Soviet vessel to enter the Cutty Sark Tall Ships' Races. Not only did she win her class, she was also awarded the coveted Cutty Sark Trophy.

*Kruzenshtern* is the second largest sailing vessel in commission and is a regular participant in the Cutty Sark Tall Ships' Races.

## DATA

Year built: 1926
Rig: 4-masted barque
Max length: 113.5m
Length of hull: 104.2m
Max height: 51.3m
Beam: 13.9m
Draught: 6.9m

Sail area: 3,023m²
Tonnage: 5,750 displacement; 3,185 tm
Crew complement: 232
Owner: Higher Kaliningrad Marine Engineering College, Russia
Construction: Steel
Builder: J.D. Tecklenborg, Wesermünde, Germany
Engine: 2 x 800 b.h.p. diesel

Photograph: Janka Bielak

# MIR

Sister ship to *Dar Mlodziezy*, *Mir* was also built at the Gdansk shipyard, and was apparently commissioned by the Soviet Union in a trading deal with Poland, along with four other sisters. She, *Druzhba*, *Khersones* and *Nadezhda* are virtually identical whilst *Pallada* has been given a black hull with a distinctive white stripe and gun port markings. *Pallada* is probably the prettiest of the Zygmant Choren B-95 types because her deck is not so encumbered with the large modern lifeboats as she has more traditional boats and life-rafts.

*Mir* and her four later sisters have a smaller spanker than the original *Dar Mlodziezy*, which is able to be eased out further thus becoming more efficient when sailing 'off the wind'. Their hulls are modern and unusual with an angular stern which, although efficient, is not as kindly on the eyes as a more traditional sailing ship hull. Their accommodation is also to a modern standard; instead of an open-plan berth deck where the entire ship's complement of trainees might live, they have sub-divided cabins for their watches. This is a great advantage to the trainees as they will, of course, be on watch at different times throughout the day and night.

*Mir* has entered more Cutty Sark Races than her sisters with the exception of *Dar Mlodziezy*. Her regular captain, Victor Antonov, is also a highly successful yacht skipper and displays many small boat skills on his big ship. During the second race of the 1989 series from Hamburg to Malmo, he 'short tacked' this majestic vessel all the way up the Jutland peninsular, only ordering the helm to be put over when the echo sounder indicated that there were only a few metres under the keel. He won his class in this race as he has won many others.

## DATA

| | |
|---|---|
| Year built: 1988 | Sail area: 3,066.5m² |
| Rig: Full-rigged ship | Tonnage: 2,385 grt |
| Max length: 109.2m | Crew complement: 194 |
| Length of hull: 94.2m | Owner: State Maritime Academy, St Petersburg, Russia |
| Max height: 50.1m | Construction: Steel |
| Beam: 13.9m | Builder: Gdansk Shipyard, Poland |
| Draught: 6.3m | Engine: 2 x 750 b.h.p. diesel |

Photograph: Cutty Sark Scots Whisky

# SEDOV

The mighty *Sedov* was launched in 1921 as *Magadelene Vinner* to carry nitrate. At that time she was unusual in that she had an auxiliary engine which would have assisted her whilst manouvering in and out of port. Her sheer size and strength would have been a comfort to her original crew who had to brave Cape Horn when bringing back nitrate from Chile and later grain from Australia. In 1936 she was sold to another German shipping company and renamed *Kommodore Johnsen* and her complement of crew under training was increased to around one hundred. At the outbreak of war in 1939 she ceased carrying cargo and took up duties as a school ship. She was handed over to the Soviet Union after the war and renamed after the famous Artic explorer, Georgy Sedov, and continued her duties as a naval school ship, training naval cadets and officers of the USSR. In 1965 her ownership was transferred to the immense Soviet Ministry of Fisheries in order to train and provide their cadets and officers with a sound training in seamanship, navigation and all aspects of seagoing life.
Following a major refit, after she had been laid up for a decade since 1971, she continued her role as a sail training ship and her début at a Cutty Sark Races event came in 1982 when she visited the fleet in Southampton. Although she did not actually race that year she returned to the races in 1986 and has been a regular participant in them ever since. Her ownership has recently been changed to the Kaliningrad Higher Marine Engineering College, who have been subsidizing her operational costs by taking on civilians from Germany and other nationals who wish to experience the exhilaration of sailing on the largest square-rigger afloat today.

## DATA

| | |
|---|---|
| Year built: 1920 | Sail area: 3,971.1m² |
| Rig: Full-rigged ship | Tonnage: 3,709 grt |
| Max length: 122.3m | Crew complement: 193 |
| Length of hull: 108.7m | Owner: Higher Kaliningrad Marine Engineering College, Russia |
| Max height: 53.5m | Construction: Steel |
| Beam: 14.2m | Builder: Krupp, Kiel, Germany |
| Draught: 6.5m | Engine: 1,180 b.h.p. diesel |

Photograph: Janka Bielak

# JUAN SEBASTIAN DE ELCANO

This magnificent four-masted schooner, which was built to train midshipmen of the Spanish navy, is named in honour of the Spanish mariner who completed the first circumnavigation in 1522 in Magellan's expedition. This famous Spanish mariner was in command of *Vittoria* when Magellan was killed during the attack on Macton in the Philippines whilst helping the king of Cebu conquer his neighbouring island. This treacherous king then murdered the two admirals elected to take Magellan's place, and de Elcano took command of the expedition, which reached Seville in 1522 with only one ship surviving out of the original fleet of five which had set out in 1519.

Launched in March 1927, she has a younger near sister *Esmeralda*. Both were designed by the British designers Camper and Nicholson, famous for the designs of the racing J Class yachts which were in their epoch during this time. She mainly differs from her sister in two respects – she is a topsail schooner as she does carry fore and aft rig on her foremast, and her fo'c's'le is shorter with two drawn deckhouses aft and forward of the poop deck.

She was the flagship of the Columbus fleet in 1992 when the main race across the Atlantic started from her home port of Cadiz.

The Spanish navy still believe that there is no real substitute for training under sail for breeding qualities of leadership, teambuilding and traditional seamanship. With over sixty training voyages and seven circumnavigations, it seems very appropriate that this fine ship should be named after such an intrepid maritime adventurer.

## DATA

| | |
|---|---|
| Year built: 1927 | Sail area: 2,775m² |
| Rig: 4-masted topsail schooner | Tonnage: 2,478 grt |
| Max length: 106.8m | Crew complement: 163 |
| Length of hull: 92.9m | Owner: Spanish Navy |
| Max height: 49.55m | Construction: Steel |
| Beam: 13.4m | Builder: Echevarrieta y Larriñaga, Cadiz, Spain |
| Draught: 6.9m | Engine: 1,500 b.h.p. diesel |

Photograph: Janka Bielak

# BLUE CLIPPER

A considerable amount of research into classic schooner design went into this carefully thought out ship, and the beautifully appointed wooden interior is a statement of excellence by Swedish and Danish craftsmen. Comfort and style on board a sailing ship of classic character which incorporated high modern safety standards was the design brief for the naval architects, and there is no doubt that this has been achieved.

Some would say that she is a development of the two-masted schooner sisters *Gladan* and *Falken*, and there is no doubting her pedigree as she has already recorded a credible noon to noon run of 265 nautical miles which is an average of over 11 knots.

Essentially operated as a chartership, her most notable voyage to date, which started in Sete and ended in Shanghai, has been under the sponsored name of *Spirit of Hennessy*. This commemorated the company's first delivery of cognac to China 120 years ago. On her return to Europe she competed in the exclusive 'La Nioulargue' event which is the annual gathering of classic yachts in St Tropez. Although none of the large square-riggers attend, this event probably attracts more of the finest classic sailing yachts in the world than any other event, and was started as a bet between the owners of two yachts to race around La Nioulargue buoy which lies twelve miles off St Tropez.

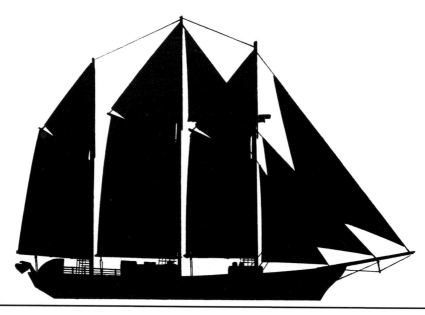

## DATA

| | |
|---|---|
| Year built: 1990 | Sail area: 650m² |
| Rig: 3-masted schooner | Tonnage: 137 grt |
| Max length: 44.00m | Crew complement: 22 |
| Length of hull: 32.14m | Owner: Blue Clipper KB |
| Max height: 32.00m | Construction: Steel |
| Beam: 7.40m | Builder: Marstrandsverken FEAB, Marstrand, Sweden |
| Draught: 3.80m | Engine: 315 b.h.p. Caterpillar |

Photograph: Blue Clipper

# GLADAN & FALKEN

Since 1556, when the Royal Swedish Navy was founded by King Gustav Wasa, there has been a tradition of sailing ships training Swedish naval cadets. Amongst these ships was the classic full-rigged iron ship *Jarramas*, which was laid up in 1948 and bought by the town of Karlskrona where she can be seen to this day. Her replacement came in the shape of two beautiful schooners named *Gladan* and *Falken*, which were commissioned in 1947.

The hull shapes, with their classic spoon bow and counter stern, have all the hallmarks of a Grand Banks schooner and were designed by the Swedish naval architect Tore Herlin with this in mind (see *Creoula*). Their good sea-keeping qualities and fast hull shapes make them difficult to beat in the races and they have consequently achieved many good placings. The two sisters were amongst the first Tall Ships' Race fleet and made history when they sailed from Torbay to Lisbon in 1956. Since then they have been stalwart members of the 'family', participating in most race series, and *Gladan* holds the rare distinction of winning the Cutty Sark Trophy on two occasions.

Their well-balanced schooner rig enables the ships to be sailed well on any point of sailing – they can also set a square sail to help their performance when sailing with the wind behind them. The naval cadets usually stay on board for a month at a time and are quickly trained so that they know every inch of the 23,600 feet of rigging: which is coincidentally about the height of Mount Everest.

The cadets offer the spectator a professional display of seamanship when setting sail as all the orders are carried out by whistle.

The only recognisable difference between these twins is the sail numbers; S1 is displayed on *Gladan's* mainsail and S2 on *Falken's*.

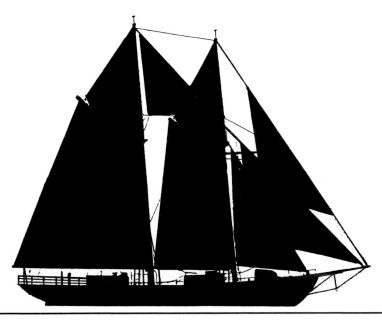

## DATA

| | |
|---|---|
| Year built: 1947 | Sail area: 638.6m² |
| Rig: Schooner | Tonnage: 220 displacement |
| Max length: 39.7m | Crew complement: 48 |
| Length of hull: 34.3m | Owner: Royal Swedish Navy |
| Max height: 31.4m | Construction: Steel |
| Beam: 7.3m | Builder: Naval Dockyard, Stockholm, Sweden |
| Draught: 4.1m | Engine: 125 b.h.p. diesel |

Photograph: Janka Bielak

# TOVARISHCH

Although *Tovarishch* has changed her nationality to Ukrainian since the breakup of the Soviet Union, she has kept her name, which is Russian for 'comrade'.

The first of the Blohm and Voss sisters (*Eagle*, *Mircea II*, *Sagres* and *Gorch Fock II*), she was built as *Gorch Fock I* to replace the barque *Niobe*. This fine ship tragically went under during a vicious squall off the Fehmarn Belt with only the captain surviving out of a crew of seventy. She differs from her sisters in that she is the only one to set a double spanker, although she was originally designed to carry a single.

She was re-engined in 1942 with a more powerful engine so that she would be better suited to her war-time role and, although she was scuttled in 1945 so that she could not be used by the Allies, in 1948 she was refloated by the Soviet Union and taken to East Germany for renovation.

In 1953 she was renamed *Tovarishch* after her predecessor, the former 2,301-ton barque *Lauriston* built in Belfast in 1892. Since then she has been training officers and cadets of the Soviet navies and she continues to train their naval personnel. She is a regular participant in the Cutty Sark Tall Ships' Races.

## DATA

| | |
|---|---|
| Year built: 1938 | Sail area: 1,930.7m² |
| Rig: Barque | Tonnage: 1,392 grt |
| Max length: 78.61m | Crew complement: 185 |
| Length of hull: 73.02m | Owner: Nautical Preparatory College, Kherson, Ukraine |
| Max height: 42.8m | Construction: Steel |
| Beam: 11.79m | Builder: Blohm & Voss, Hamburg, Germany |
| Draught: 4.75m | Engine: 550 b.h.p. diesel |

Photograph: Janka Bielak

# ASTRID

Constructed in the Netherlands at the end of the First World War, she started life as a trading schooner with the name of *Wuta*. This is appropriately short for: 'Wacht uw tiyd af' ('Be patient, wait for better times').

Still under Dutch command and ownership, in 1934 her rig was reduced to that of a Vracht-Logger until 1937 when she was sold to a Swedish farmer and renamed *Astrid*. She remained under his ownership for thirty-nine years trading in wheat, barley and rape-seed with the Scandinavian countries, and during the Second World War she carried timber and coal between Sweden and Poland.

Probably her most infamous period followed in 1976 when *Astrid* was sold and registered under the Lebanese ensign. This dark period of the old lady's life ended in the English Channel on 13 July 1977 when Her Majesty's Customs Officers, suspecting her of smuggling drugs, demanded to board her. The guilty crew soaked her accommodation in petrol and set her ablaze, and by the following morning two bodies were recovered from the floating debris. Three others were still unaccounted for when she was towed into Newhaven.

In 1984, realizing her great potential as a sail training vessel for young people, Commander Graham Nielson bought the neglected hull and started the massive renovation which was to take four years. Since then, every winter, she has been giving many young people an opportunity of 'signing on for a long voyage of personal discovery' across the Atlantic. Not only do her crew have to master the gruelling day-to-day duties of running a traditional sailing ship, but they have many other tasks such as taking scientific samples from the ocean and monitoring all the instruments of this official weather ship.

A regular participant of the Cutty Sark Tall Ships' Races, *Astrid* is a popular member of the international 'family'.

## DATA

| | |
|---|---|
| Year built: 1918 | Sail area: 449.9m² |
| Rig: Brig | Tonnage: 170 grt |
| Max length: 41.36m | Crew complement: 34 |
| Length of hull: 33.07m | Owner: Astrid Trust, Weymouth, Dorset, UK |
| Max height: 27.0m | Construction: Iron |
| Beam: 6.61m | Builder: Greg van Leeuwen, Scheveningen, Holland |
| Draught: 2.48m | Engine: Scania 290 b.h.p. diesel |

Photograph: Janka Bielak

# LORD NELSON

*Lord Nelson* was the first sailing ship in the world to be designed to carry physically handicapped people as half its crew complement. This presented a difficult challenge for her designer Colin Mudie, FRINA. He needed to incorporate the stringent safety regulations laid down by the Department of Transport, together with the many built-in facilities to help the physically handicapped crew perform their duties alongside their able-bodied shipmates, without taking away the element of challenge.

The result has proved to be tremendously successful. She has many navigational aids, which include an audio compass for the blind and visual displays and signal systems for the deaf. Her decks are all level with lifts to enable those crew who are confined to wheelchairs to move around and join in with the running of the ship. Her fore and aft sails are self-furling and the topgallants and royals furl into the yards.

Although she was built as recently as 1986, *Lord Nelson* has covered many miles, and with her double transatlantic crossing in 1989, she has proved to be a very seaworthy vessel. She is a loyal supporter of the Cutty Sark Tall Ships' Races and she has acted as the communications ship in 1989 and 1991.

## DATA

Year built: 1984/86
Rig: Barque
Max length: 51.07m
Length of hull: 42.98m
Max height: 32.0m
Beam: 8.53m
Draught: 4.12m

Sail area: 1,000m²
Tonnage: 400 displacement
Crew complement: 50
Owner: Jubilee Sailing Trust, UK
Construction: Steel
Builder: James Cook & Co, Wyvenhoe/Vosper Thornycroft, UK
Engine: 2 x 260 b.h.p. diesel

Photograph: Cutty Sark Scots Whisky

# ROYALIST

The keel of this delightful brig was laid down on Trafalgar Day 1970 and she was launched by H.R.H Princess Anne in 1971. She is probably one of the most perfectly designed sail training ships of recent years and fulfils her role magnificently. She won the Lloyds Register Yacht Award that year, which essentially means that she was considered the 'best constructed and best equipped vessel for its purpose'.

She was built at Groves and Guttridge on the Isle of Wight but, although she looks traditional, her innovative design was the product of considerable wind tunnel and tank testing. Modern materials were also used in her construction and with a high degree of safety equipment, twin engines and stability curves extending over 90 degrees, she is a very safe ship.

Much attention was also given to the ergonomics of living conditions on board. The brig is virtually decked throughout with teak, and the bulkheads and deckheads are lined in modern laminates for a smart appearance and ease of maintenance. Each cadet has their own bunk and kit-locker. With central heating, a fridge and freezer, she is a most comfortable sail training ship.

She is operated by the British Sea Cadet Corps and generally enters the Cutty Sark Tall Ships' Races. The Sea Cadet Corps's first entry in the races was in 1966 when they were lent the brigantine *Centurion* to enter the race from Falmouth to the Skaw and won.

When racing today, she often is very close to her friendly rival *Asgard II*, which has a similar turn of speed and Time Correction Factor.

Varuna

The Indian Sea Cadet Corps commissioned a sistership to be built in 1971, identical except that *Varuna* has a white hull with black painted false gun ports, which is the reverse to her sister.

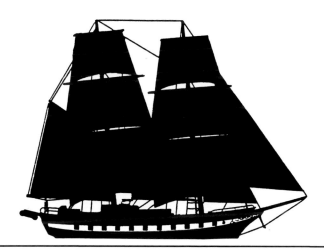

## DATA

| | |
|---|---|
| Year built: 1971 | Sail area: 433m² |
| Rig: Brig | Tonnage: 90 displacement |
| Max length: 28.07m | Crew complement: 33 |
| Length of hull: 23.17m | Owner: Sea Cadet Corps, UK |
| Max height: 24.3m | Construction: Steel |
| Beam: 6.10m | Builder: Groves & Guttridge, Cowes, UK |
| Draught: 2.74m | Engine: 2 x 230 b.h.p. Perkins, diesel |

Photograph: Cutty Sark Scots Whisky

# SIR WINSTON CHURCHILL

Due to the success of the International Tall Ships' Races, the STA decided to build a 235-ton displacement, three-masted topsail schooner *Sir Winston Churchill* which was launched in 1966. She was designed by Camper and Nicholson in association with the famous ocean racer Captain John Illingworth, and was based on the successful 166-foot schooner *Sonia II*. Her internal layout is arranged to accommodate thirty-nine trainees who are organised into three watches. The permanent afterguard consists of a master, chief officer, bosun, engineer and cook, and for each voyage a voluntary navigator, a purser, three watch officers and three watch leaders are taken on. Her success prompted a sistership to be built in 1968, *Malcolm Miller*. She differs only slightly on deck by having square-shaped top deckhouse doors, and below decks by having small improvements to her engine room and accommodation. The building was funded largely by Sir James Miller in memory of his son who was killed in a gliding accident.

Since 1966, the two schooners have taken over 28,000 young people to sea, giving them an unforgettable experience that has often proved a formative influence in their lives. Their aim is to help youngsters learn about themselves, their capabilities and awareness of others. The emphasis is on the social experience, no attempt is made to turn them into yachtsmen or professional seaman, although the trainees participate fully in the running of the ship.

These sleek vessels are ardent supporters of the Cutty Sark Tall Ships' Races and each are crewed by a male and a female crew complement. This often results in some very competitive ocean racing between the two schooners.

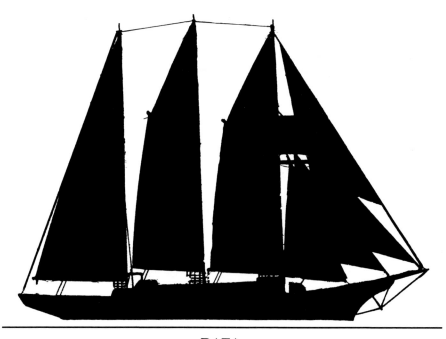

## DATA

| | |
|---|---|
| Year built: 1966/1968 | Tonnage: 218.46 grt |
| Rig: Topsail schooner | Crew complement: 55 |
| Max length: 45.32m | Owner: Sail Training Association, Schooners, Portsmouth, |
| Length of hull: 41.06m | UK |
| Max height: 33.42m | Construction: Steel |
| Beam: 7.62m | Builder: R. Dunston, Hull, UK (Sir Winston Churchill) |
| Draught: 4.43m | John Lewis & Sons Ltd, Aberdeen, UK (Malcolm Miller) |
| Sail area: 814.9m² | Engine: 2 x 135 b.h.p. Perkins, diesel |

Photograph: Cutty Sark Scots Whisky

# SOREN LARSEN

*Soren Larsen* was one of the last sailing vessels to trade under sail in the Baltic and North Sea carrying timber, wheat and beans amongst a variety of other cargoes. She was built as a three-masted schooner in 1948 at the Lymfjord port of Nykobing and traded until 1972 when she was decommissioned.

In 1978 this Scandinavian 'lady' was bought by a company named Squaresail and was extensively refitted and converted into a delightful brigantine. She became a television celebrity overnight when she starred in the popular BBC drama series The Onedin Line. Her stardom continued when she featured in films such as The French Lieutenant's Woman, Rights of Passage, Count of Monte Cristo and Dick Turpin.

In 1983 she entered her first Cutty Sark Tall Ships' Race under the flag of the Jubilee Sailing Trust, and was awarded the Cutty Sark Wheel Trophy for her contribution to international understanding and friendship.* She continued with the JST for two years taking disabled people to sea with the idea of developing systems and methods which could be incorporated into *Lord Nelson*.

She became the flagship of a group of vessels which re-enacted the voyage of the 'First Fleet' when they sailed to Australia via Rio, Capetown and Mauritius. They arrived to a tumultuous welcome in Sydney harbour on 26 January 1988, two hundred years after the First Fleet. After the celebrations she continued voyaging in the Southern Hemisphere until she joined the Columbus Regatta in Lisbon via Cape Horn.

\* Until 1989 the main races were only held every other year and a minor race was staged in between. The Cutty Sark Trophy was therefore only awarded during the major races and the Cutty Sark Wheel and Bell trophies were presented for the minor races.

## DATA

| | |
|---|---|
| Year built: 1949 | Sail area: 736.2m² |
| Rig: Brigantine | Tonnage: 149 grt |
| Max length: 40.70m | Crew complement: 40 |
| Length of hull: 31.61m | Owner: Tony Davis, Squaresail, UK |
| Max height: 29.69m | Construction: Wood |
| Beam: 7.77m | Builder: Soren Larsen Shipyard, Nykobing, Denmark |
| Draught: 3.12m | Engine: 240 b.h.p. diesel |

Photograph: Max

# EAGLE

Commissioned in 1936 as the *Horst Wessel* after a young Nazi leader, she was one of three sisterships to be built by Blohm and Voss. These fine three-masted barques were operated by the growing German navy to train their young cadets. In the early part of World War II, she was converted into a cargo ship and transported men and supplies throughout the Baltic Sea. During this period the legend goes that her guns downed three Russian planes, and she had a lucky escape towards the end of the war, when off Kiel her captain altered course to Flensburg avoiding a most devastating air raid.

Another feat of survival came in 1946, when she was caught in a hurricane during her passage to her new home in the United States. Since then she has been successfully training cadets of the US Coast Guard and voyaging annually to Europe or the Caribbean. Her trainees have a demanding time on board, having to master the disciplines of navigation, seamanship and engineering, as well as putting into practice many hours of theory which they have previously learnt in the classroom.

Her three sisters are still in commission and engaged in very similar training roles. *Tovarishch*, originally built as *Gorch Fock I* in 1933, is operated by the Ukrainian Republic. The Portuguese naval barque *Sagres II*, was launched in 1938 with the name of *Albert Leo Schlageter*, and her near sistership *Mircea II* is under the Romanian ensign.

## DATA

| | |
|---|---|
| Year built: 1936 | Sail area: 2,129.9m² |
| Rig: Barque | Tonnage: 1,634 displacement |
| Max length: 89.52m | Crew complement: 209 |
| Length of hull: 81.32m | Owner: United States Coastguard |
| Max height: 46.3m | Construction: Steel |
| Beam: 12.01m | Builder: Blohm & Voss, Hamburg, Germany |
| Draught: 4.88m | Engine: 750 b.h.p. diesel |

Photograph: Alexander Bielak

# PRIDE OF BALTIMORE II

Baltimore clippers were designed at the time of the Revolutionary War with one thing in mind – speed. The young American navy consisted of only four frigates until well into the nineteenth century and offered little protection to the merchant marine. These fleet-footed schooners, with their raked masts and clouds of sail, were therefore designed to out-run the many pirates and foreign warships which worked the east coast of America.

These clippers had various roles to play in the history of the USA, from revenue cutters to privateers as well as merchant ships, and flourished until the 1812 war. Their slim hull design meant that they had a limited cargo space which made them unprofitable to operate. Consequently the larger Yankee clippers evolved in the mid-nineteenth century.

*Pride of Baltimore II* was built in 1988 to carry on the role of the original working replica, which was tragically lost in May 1986 when she was knocked flat by a freak squall and sank within minutes. Her principal role is to serve as 'a world class economic development and goodwill ambassador for the state of Maryland and the Port of Baltimore'. She has unlimited certification and can sail anywhere in the world. It is traditional when she visits Britain to challenge one of the STA schooners to race in Weymouth Bay and, although she is the smaller ship, she has the edge in most sailing conditions.

The *Pride* has also evolved as a valuable educational resource. The 'Students with Pride' programme links Maryland students with their counterparts from all over the globe, and together they study a curriculum of geography, maths, science and history based on the *Pride*'s travels. The crew stay in contact with other students via the latest in satellite and fax technology.

The permanent crew of twelve can take up to thirty-five guests on a day sail reception and 125 guests when entertaining alongside in harbour. The professional crew members are largely made up of young men and women who sign up for six or nine months, while the two captains rotate every three or four months.

## DATA

| | |
|---|---|
| Year built: 1988 | Sail area: 971.3m² |
| Rig: 2-masted topsail schooner | Tonnage: 185.5 displacement |
| Max length: 43.28m | Crew complement: 12 |
| Length of hull: 31.09m | Owner: Pride of Baltimore Inc, USA |
| Beam: 7.95m | Construction: Wood |
| Draught: 3.75m | Builder: G. Peter Boudreau |
| | Engine: 2 x Caterpillar turbo 140 b.h.p. diesel |

Photograph: Cutty Sark Scots Whisky

# CAPTAIN MIRANDA

*Captain Miranda* was built as a two-masted hydrographic vessel at the Makagorda shipyard in Cadiz during 1930, and for forty years she charted the shores, islands, reefs and bays of Uruguay. Condemned to the scrapyard, she was reprieved in 1977 and converted into a sail training ship for the Uruguayan navy as a three-masted schooner. During the conversion a staggering 120 square metres of metal plating on the hull was renewed and the old 25-ton engine was replaced with a modern V12 cylinder type of only six tons. Reinforced concrete and wrought iron had to be installed in the engine room in order to regain the loss of stability.

Affectionately known as the African Queen because of her graceful Edwardian lines, she gallantly represented her country 'down under' during the Australian bicentennial celebrations in 1988. She can often also be seen in northern Europe and the Baltic, participating in the Cutty Sark Tall Ships' Races or representing her country on a state visit.

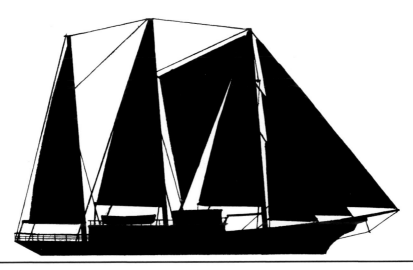

## DATA

| | |
|---|---|
| Year built: 1930 | Sail area: 746.4m² |
| Rig: Schooner | Tonnage: 600 displacement |
| Max length: 60.44m | Crew complement: 102 |
| Length of hull: 53.45m | Owner: Uruguayan Navy |
| Max height: 38.44m | Construction: Steel |
| Beam: 8.0m | Builder: Makagorda Shipyard, Cadiz, Spain |
| Draught: 3.6m | Engine: V12 diesel |

Photograph: Janka Bielak

# SIMON BOLIVAR

Built for the Venezuelan navy in 1979, this white-hulled, three-masted barque has clean lines which are complemented by a line of black false gun ports, so she is easily identified. She is from the same Spanish shipyard as *Gloria*, *Guayas* and *Cuauhtemoc*. All are different in size and layout but they have many similarities and share the same pedigree. *Simon Bolivar* is larger than her predecessors, has a transom stern and is more traditional as she does not sport a forward bridge.

She is patriotically named after General Simon Bolivar, 'El Liberator' who drove the Spanish out of South America gaining independence for Venezuela, Peru, Colombia, Bolivia and Ecuador. She carries a figurehead in his honour.

Her first Tall Ships' Race was in 1984 when she joined the transatlantic fleet in Bermuda (after competing in the feeder race from Puerto Rico) and raced to Halifax. She then cruised-in-company to Gaspe and Quebec. She has maintained a high international profile by participating in Sail Amsterdam in 1985, the Statue of Liberty centenary celebrations in 1986, the Australian bicentennial celebrations in 1988 and the Columbus Regatta in 1992.

## DATA

| | |
|---|---|
| Year built: 1979 | Sail area: 1,978.2m² |
| Rig: Barque | Tonnage: 934 grt |
| Max length: 82.30m | Crew complement: 194 |
| Length of hull: 68.60m | Owner: Venezuelan Navy |
| Max height: 38.9m | Construction: Steel |
| Beam: 10.60m | Builder: ASTACE, Bilbao, Spain |
| Draught: 4.41m | Engine: 750 b.h.p. diesel |

Photograph: Janka Bielak
Photograph overleaf: Janka Bielak

# HOW TO SAIL ON THE TALL SHIPS

Anyone between the ages of sixteen and twenty-five (inclusive) can sail in the Cutty Sark Tall Ships' Races – it is a rule of entry that at least 50% of the ship's total crew complement need to be in this age bracket. If you are above twenty-five and have some sailing experience, you can apply to sail as part of the afterguard – if not, there are many organisations which provide excellent programmes for enthusiastic volunteers who wish to train and develop their skills for future races.

An ASTO (Association of Sea Training Organisations) leaflet, which has outline information on costs, contact addresses and telephone numbers of the recognised British sail training organisations, can be obtained from the following address. (Please enclose a stamped addressed envelope):

ASTO
c/o The Sail Training Association
5 Mumby Road
Gosport
Hants PO12 1AA

The Members of ASTO are:

Cirdan Trust
Excelsior Trust
Fairbridge
Faramir Trust
Island Cruising Club
Joint Services Adventurous Sail Training Centre
Jubilee Sailing Trust
London Sailing Project
Morning Star Trust
Ocean Youth Club
Sail Training Association Schooners
Scouts Offshore
Sea Cadet Corps
Shaftesbury Homes and *Arethusa*

ASTO was formed in 1960 and is the co-ordinating body of the recognised British sail training organisations.

Many of the ASTO members will be entering their vessels in the Cutty Sark Tall Ships' Races, but it is best to contact them as soon as possible as the berths on the races are very popular and are booked early. In addition, each offers a comprehensive programme of sail training voyages for the young person or adult.

There are similar national bodies in other European and Scandinavian countries, many are affiliated to the STA and have dual roles in supporting their own sail training schemes as well as being involved with the Tall Ships' Races. The principal organisations are:

Photograph opposite: Cutty Sark Scots Whisky

**Aporvela**
*Caleada Palma de Baixo 4–8F*
1600 Lisbon
Portugal

**The American Sail Training Association**
PO Box 1459
Newport
RI 02840
USA

**STA Finland**
c/o Kotkan Satamalaitos
Laivurinkatu 7
48100 Kotka
Finland

**STA Germany**
D–2850 Bremerhaven – F
AM Hollwerk 1
Germany

**STA Japan**
Nanyo-do Bldg
2F 1-14-4 Hongo
Bunkyo-ku
Tokyo
Japan

**STA Netherlands**
Postbus 55
2340 AB Oegstgeest
Netherlands

**STA Poland**
Gdynska Fundacja Zeglarska
al. Zjednoczenia 3
81-963 Gdynia 1
Poland

**STA Russia**
St Petersburg Engineering
   Marine College
Kosaya Line 15a
Russia

# OCEAN YOUTH CLUB

Europe's largest sail training organisation

## The Aims

OYC exists to provide equality of opportunity for all young people to develop responsibility and knowledge about themselves, others and society.

The enjoyment and adventure of life at sea can help young people learn:

- A sense of equality and fairness
- An understanding of the needs and different backgrounds of others
- Responsibility for their own decisions and actions
- Teamwork and mutual trust
- Awareness of the environment
- As well as the obvious range of sea, sailing and survival skills.

The Club aims to involve young people from as wide a range of backgrounds as possible, and to take crews mixed by sex, ability and ethnic origin. Thus, young people from comfortable middle class backgrounds learn to live and work with the socially and physically disadvantaged. In 1992 *Lady Beaverbrook* participated in the Columbus Regatta with deaf and partially sighted young people on board, and in Northern Ireland the Oyster 68 *Lord Rank* has been providing positive evidence that sailing with the OYC encourages mutual understanding between young people from all communities.

It is the Club's proud boast that no young person who wants to sail with the OYC is unable to do so because of cost. Local and national bursary funds exist to help those with limited means, but everyone is encouraged to pay something themselves so that they feel that they have contributed. Over 60% of OYC young crews are subsidised.

## A Brief History

Founded in 1960, the OYC started with just two vessels, *Ocean Pelican* and the Bristol Channel Pilot Cutter *Equinoxe*. These Pilot Cutters are renowned for their sea keeping qualities and *Equinoxe* served the Club well. The Reverend Courtauld very generously lent the OYC his beautiful yawl *Duet* to increase the fleet to three vessels and she is still operated by the Club today!

Although no one realised it at the time, a Cornishman named Geoffrey Williams, who had just won the 1968 Observer Singlehanded Transatlantic Race in a ketch named *Sir Thomas Lipton*, would have a great influence on the Club. The 56-foot Robert Clark designed ketch stood up well to the severe weather that pounded the Observer fleet that year, and Williams decided that it would make an excellent sail training yacht with which to equip the Club for the 1970s. Amazingly, a boat-

yard was bought in Penryn and the sponsorship was raised to build eight 72-foot ketches which were based on the design of *Lipton*. By 1976 ten had been built for the Club, the prototype had been sold abroad and No. 7 was bought by Shaftesbury Homes and *Arethusa*.

These foam sandwich constructed yachts have proved to be an excellent tool for sail training and some are still in operation today. *Sir Thomas Sopwith* was sold to the Ocean Youth Club of Australia in 1987 and has since completed a circumnavigation.

In 1985 a fleet replacement programme was launched and two steel shipwright 70-foot ketches were commissioned sometime after. For many reasons this design has proved less successful but *James Cook* and *John Laing* serve the Club well.

## The Club Today

A fun adventure experience is what you are likely to get with the Ocean Youth Club. The Club has ten specifically designed sail training yachts stationed around the UK. These vessels offer an exciting opportunity to go sailing around the coasts of Europe, and sometimes more adventurous voyages are undertaken, such as across the Atlantic or to the Azores.

The OYC employs a professional skipper for each of its vessels and the watch leaders' positions are filled with voluntary qualified members. The Club is open to anyone over twelve years old; ordinary members are between the ages of twelve and twenty-four, if you are older, you are designated a 'friend' of the Club. The OYC has always been a progressive sail training organisation and is particularly suited to taking a diversity of groups or individuals. The Club has made much progress over the past few years and is developing as a youth organisation which is ensuring quality training and management of their young crews in line with the educational authorities.

Apart from a graceful eighty-year-old gaff yawl *Duet*, and *Greater Manchester Challenge*, the Club's fleet is made up of Bermudan ketches of around seventy or eighty feet taking between eighteen and twenty-five crew in total. This has proved to be a very successful size of sail training vessel as it is cost effective to operate and the young crew members can get totally involved in all aspects of running the yacht.

Each yacht's home base has a Support Group which is made up of enthusiastic members who offer support to the vessel's shoreside operation. The strength of the Club is in its members and the Support Group often also become actively involved with the yacht's winter refit.

**The Yachts**

OYC Robert Clark Ketches:
*Lady Beaverbrook*   OYC 2 (ex Falmouth Packet)
*Master Builder*   OYC 3
*Taikoo*   OYC 5
*Spirit of Boadecea*   OYC 7
*Francis Drake*   OYC 8
Length:21.79 metres
Beam:4.30 metres
Draught:2.29 metres
Sail area:213 sq metres

Shipwright Class:
*James Cook*   OYC 1
*John Laing*   OYC 6
Length: 20.95 metres
Beam: 5.42 metres
Draught: 2.60 metres
Sail area: 262 sq metres

Oyster 68:
*Lord Rank*: OYC 10
Length: 17.49 metres
Beam: 4.47 metres
Draught: 2.13 metres
Sail area: 182 sq metres

Oyster 80 (Planned to be built 1995)
Length: 24.05 metres
Beam: 5.79 metres
Draught: 2.69 metres

Other Classes:
*Greater Manchester Challenge* (OYC 12)
Length: 20.50 metres
Beam: 5.34 metres
Draught: 2.60 metres
Sail area: 289 sq metres

Photograph: Cutty Sark Scots Whisky

# LONDON SAILING PROJECT

## The Aims

'The London Sailing Project is an organisation whose aim is to provide opportunities for London boys to acquire those attributes of a seaman, namely a sense of responsibility, resourcefulness and teamwork which will stay with them throughout their lives.'

## How it all began

'The Project' or 'LSP', as it is known within sail training circles, began during the time of Harold Macmillan's government when The Right Honourable Derek Heathcoat Amory was Chancellor of the Exchequer. Because of his ministerial duties, he never knew whether he would be free to go sailing at the weekend on board his yacht *Ailanthus*. Heathcoat Amory therefore invited Commander Walter Scott and his Stepney Sea Scouts to use *Ailanthus* which meant that, whether he had any last minute official engagements or not, the yacht would go sailing anyway, providing the young scouts with an excellent opportunity. By 1959 this arrangement had proved so successful that it was decided to formally establish the London Project and by 1961 a 75-foot ketch named *Rona* was purchased for a mere £6,625.

## Operational Details

Since that time the LSP has increased its permanent fleet to three yachts and has moved its operations base from Gosport to the river Hamble. The strength of the LSP is that it is largely a self-generating organisation as many of its volunteer skippers, mates, watch officers and watch leaders started out as 'boys'. Consequently, this means that there is a considerable amount of dedication and enthusiasm within the organisation and the voyage fees remain low.

The LSP runs weekend or weekly voyages from March to November and has now broadened its trainee recruitment from outside London. During a week-long voyage from the Hamble the yacht is likely to visit the north coast of France, the Channel Islands and a couple of ports on the south coast of the UK. However, the highlight of the sailing season is when one of the yachts participates in the Cutty Sark Tall Ships' Races, and the crew have often gained line honours in a fleet of nearly one hundred vessels.

In 1976 the LSP chartered Chay Blyth's maxi *Great Britain II* directly after she had arrived back from winning the Financial Times Clipper Race, and entered her in the STA American Bicentennial

Photograph: Cutty Sark Scots Whisky

Tall Ships' Race. Many sceptical ocean racers said that a maxi could not be handled by such a young crew, but the Project proved them wrong and they went on to arrive first in the Canaries, Bermuda and Plymouth. Since then, they have successfully entered two more transatlantic races in 1984 and 1992 with their ketches *Donald Searle* and *Rona II*.

During an LSP voyage some of the twelve trainees might be awarded an Amory award, which is presented to those youngsters 'which gave their best' – they are then automatically invited onto the watch leader's selection weekend. If they are fortunate enough to pass they will then sail as one of three watch leaders on a voyage, organising a team of four new recruits with duties like sail changes and the washing up! In time, when they have proved themselves as a good leader and have gained sufficient experience and qualifications, they will then be promoted to a watch officer. The watch officer in turn directs the watch leader as well as ensuring a good look-out is kept and the yacht is sailed efficiently. Eventually, the watch officer may be promoted to the mate, who is the skipper's right hand man and could, if necessary, take over command.

**The Yachts**

*Rona II*
The newest of the three yachts, *Rona II* was built in 1992 from the standard Oyster 68 hull and deck. She is vastly different below however, as the usual Oyster 68 would be built for the discerning private owner or charter company and would be appointed to a very high standard. She takes a total of 20 crew.
Year built: 1991
Rig: Bermudan Ketch
Length: 20.57 metres
Beam: 5.26 metres
Draught: 1.95 metres
Sail area: 257 sq metres

*Donald Searle*
A well proven sail training vessel, *Donald Searle* has a standard Ocean 75 hull. The deck has been modified by removing the secondary cockpit, as it was found that this was a very popular place to hide when the less enthusiastic crew members wanted to avoid certain duties. As with *Rona II* she also has a total complement of 20.
Year built: 1979
Rig: Bermudan ketch
Length: 22.89 metres
Beam: 5.30 metres
Draught: 2.59 metres
Sail area: 309 sq metres

*Helen Mary R*
This ketch shares the same hull and deck design as *Debenhams*, which was the yacht in which John Ridgeway participated in the Whitbread Round the World Race and later broke the global non-stop record. This Bowman 57 seldom ventures abroad as her role is to take the fifteen-year-old LSP boys to sea. Being almost ten tons lighter, her gear is significantly easier to handle but it still takes close teamwork to sail a yacht like this well.
Year built: 1986
Rig: Bermudan ketch
Length: 17.49 metres
Beam: 4.47 metres
Draught: 2.13 metres
Sail area: 182 sq metres

# MORNING STAR TRUST

The Morning Star Trust is a Christian sail training organisation based in Chatham Historic Dockyard on the River Medway. The Trust operates a 62-foot gaff-rigged ketch *Morning Star of Revelation* which takes groups of young people sailing in the Thames Estuary and North Sea, and also competes annually in the Cutty Sark Tall Ships' Races.

With her gaff ketch rig, she is an ideal small training vessel and is unusually constructed of ferro-cement to a good standard. She accommodates fourteen persons in three cabins of four, with a separate cabin for the skipper and the mate. She is a well-proven vessel, having completed many tens of thousands of miles since she was launched in 1980.

Sailing on *Morning Star* is aimed at being challenging and enjoyable whilst providing the opportunity to learn a range of sailing and seamanship skills. The Trust aims to help people to:

– Gain in confidence, overcome fears and learn to trust
– Discover and develop their gifts as individuals
– Learn their value in a team.

The Trust also operate a Halcyon 27, *Eagle Wings*, which enables their more enthusiastic experienced young sailors to develop their skills, become qualified and then to sail as second mate, first mate or even skipper on their larger *Morning Star of Revelation*.

# SHAFTESBURY HOMES AND *ARETHUSA*

### A Short History

The Shaftesbury Homes and *Arethusa* were founded in 1843 by William Williams who worked extensively with pauper and orphan children. In 1866, at the suggestion of the 7th Earl of Shaftesbury, a training ship *HMS Chichester* was established at Greenhithe on the River Thames. Destitute children were given a proper education there with a good knowledge of seamanship and navigation to aid their entry into the Royal Navy.

The moorings were moved to Lower Upnor on the River Medway in 1932 when the Society acquired the ex-Flying P four-masted barque *Peking* which was renamed *Arethusa*.

Close scrutiny of the Society's sea training programme in relation to the needs of future young people brought about a radical change in the type of vessel that was to replace *Peking*, after her sale to the New York Sea Museum in 1974. A 72-foot Bermudan ketch was commissioned in 1975 to allow hundreds of young people from disadvantaged backgrounds to experience the benefits of personal development which the sea can offer. This vessel, which was the third *Arethusa*, was the seventh Robert Clark designed OYC ketch and was later sold back to the OYC and renamed *Spirit of Boadicea* and is still operating today.

### The Work of *Arethusa*

The wooden David Cannel designed ketch, which was completed by trainee boatbuilders at Lowerstoft in 1982, competed in her first Cutty Sark Tall Ships' Race that year. The finishing touches to the building programme were actually carried out by the crew on the race across the Bay of Biscay!

She generally works a weekly sail training programme taking groups of young people from mainly disadvantaged backgrounds and inner-city areas. Her weekly voyages involve a visit to France, Belgium or Holland and the young crew become totally integrated in the daily shipboard routine of navigation, helming, sail handling and watch keeping as well as the daily domestic chores of cooking and cleaning. In addition, during the summer holidays individuals, schools and other youth activity groups get the opportunity of sailing this impressive ketch. During the winter months she sometimes sails to warmer climes like the Canary Islands, which helps offset the high operating costs of a sail training yacht.

The voyages do not aim necessarily to teach the crew how to sail, although many of the keener ones do learn a great deal, but they help to develop individual achievement, personal self esteem and team work through facing a difficult and demanding environment together.

A dedicated member of the 'family', *Arethusa* has participated in almost every Cutty Sark Tall Ships' Race since she was launched.

# SEA CADET CORPS

In 1856, sailors returning from the Crimean War established the Naval Lads Brigade in Whitstable, and by the turn of the century several other towns had their own training brigs and brigantines. This was the beginning of the Sea Cadet Corps and probably makes it the longest serving youth organisation in Britain.

It has developed over the many years and today has up to 20,000 boys and girls belonging to 400 units. There are also many affiliated and similar organisations from all over the world. They all have one thing in common, mainly waterborne activities which promote self-discipline and leadership qualities, which in turn develop their young members' sense of responsibility to the community. The Corps is divided into six regional areas and the activities, which are run by the individual units, include boatwork, canoeing, communications, expeditions, first aid, seamanship, meteorology and sea going voyages. The activities which the Corps provide on a national level include visits to warships, courses in RN training establishments, regattas and square-rigged sailing in their brig *Royalist*.

In addition to *Royalist* the Corps have two 43-foot wooden sloops *Martin* and *Petrel*, which operate weekly voyages around the coast of the UK and participate in the Cutty Sark Tall Ships' Races. These Morgan Giles designed yachts have offered many young sea cadets some exciting sailing in the past and continue to do so.

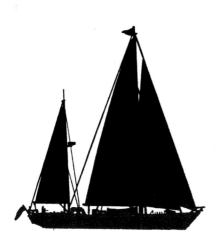

# ISLAND CRUISING CLUB

Situated in the beautiful Salcombe Estuary and founded in 1951, the Island Cruising Club offers a wide range of sailing for everyone. Its fleet consists of over fifty dinghies and keelboats which are operated from the converted Mersey ferry *Egremont*. This is now the accommodation vessel for the small boat courses and is moored towards the upper reaches of the estuary, which is designated an area of outstanding beauty.

The club operates two small yachts which are programmed to cover all the Royal Yachting Association practical cruising courses, so whether you are an experienced skipper with no certification, or have never sailed before, the ICC will be able to provide you with a suitable course to gain the appropriate qualifications.

The elegant *Hoshi*, an Edwardian gaff-rigged schooner, and *Provident*, a converted Brixham trawler, make up their larger fleet. *Hoshi* was built in 1909 by the distinguished Camper and Nicholson and was taken on by the club when it was founded. Her original sailing rig was significantly larger then than it is today. Her lead keel was sacrificed to pay for a large refit, and consequently the sail area was reduced when the less efficient internal ballast was substituted. Although it would have been a grand sight to see her with the original lofty masts and overhanging mainsail, she would probably not have survived so well because of the extra associated stresses that it would have put onto her hull. She takes nine members and a 'permanent' skipper, mate and cook.

*Provident* is also manned by a skipper, mate and cook but takes twelve members. She has benefitted from a large refit which was carried out in the mid-nineteen eighties, and also offers first-class corporate entertainment and management training facilities. These subsidise the members' cruises which are usually one week in length. They generally start and finish in Salcombe, having cruised the beautiful coast of Brittany and the delightful Channel Islands. This famous Brixham trawler entered the first Tall Ships' Race from Torbay to Lisbon in 1956 but it is *Hoshi* who usually graces the Cutty Sark fleet today.

The ICC work hand in hand with the Island Trust, which is a charitable body supported by the club. One of the first organisations to offer special courses for the visually impaired, the Trust also assists the deaf and the disadvantaged who sail with the club on their traditional vessels and sailing dinghies.

Over 2,500 people of all ages and backgrounds enjoy a holiday or course with the ICC each year, which makes it one of the largest sailing organisations in the UK.

# MARY BRYANT

This beautifully proportioned US east coast schooner, *Mary Bryant*, was designed by Murray Peterson and was launched in 1981. She made her début in 1983 when she entered the Weymouth to St Malo race and went on to enter the 1985 and 1987 races.

She now operates as a skippered charter boat and a Royal Yachting Association approved sailing school based in Falmouth. During the summer she also cruises the beautiful west coast of Scotland, and during the winter she goes off for an occasional foray to the sunshine of the Caribbean. The cruises vary in length and emphasis, some concentrate on RYA instruction, some on the wildlife of the western isles and of the west country. She continues to participate in traditional boat gatherings and plans to enter the Cutty Sark Tall Ships' Races once again in the near future.

Year built: 1981
Rig: 2-masted gaff-rigged schooner
Max length: 13.75 metres
Length deck: 12.5 metres
Max beam: 3.66 metres
Max draught: 1.83 metres
Crew Complement: 6 total
Construction: wood

*Hoshi*. Photograph: Roger Ball

# SCOUTS OFFSHORE

The Scouts Offshore was founded in 1964 and was the idea of the leader of the 12th Colchester Sea Scouts, Ken Wright. His vision was to extend the scope of the scouts' sailing activities and this he did by organising the purchase of *Sallie*, a 14-metre converted fishing smack built in 1908.

Since then the movement has gown from strength to strength and has owned an ex-Fastnet race winner *Ramrod*, a 10-metre sloop *Mersea Rival* and an Ohlson 38, *Moonshadow*. The present day fleet consists of the ex-winning Admiral's Cup yacht *Prospect of Whitby*, now named *Salex*, and a new Oyster 49 named *Ocean Scout*. The Sparkman and Stephens designed *Salex* has a tremendous pedigree as an ocean racer and offers exciting sailing for the scouts, whereas *Ocean Scout* has attributes as a comfortable cruising yacht with her large galley and refrigerator, two heads and hot and cold running water.

Although the scheme was principally established to take scouts to sea, it now also attracts many youngsters from a variety of other organisations including school parties. The scheme's aims are:

- To offer an introduction to the excitement and adventure of offshore sailing to young people from a wide range of backgrounds, including those who have special educational and social needs
- To teach the skills of seamanship; and to offer RYA practical courses in the Cruising Scheme under the direction of qualified instructors
- To create opportunities for personal development in a physically challenging environment, and to inculcate initiative and leadership skills
- To provide the basis for a communal experience on board ship in which teamwork and co-operation are at least as important as self-reliance, toughness, and individual fortitude
- To encourage an awareness of the beauty of the natural world, particularly the sea in all its changing moods, and man's place in that world.

# JOINT SERVICES ADVENTUROUS SAIL TRAINING CENTRE

The British Services operate a sail training centre in Gosport which provides adventurous training at sea for their young personnel. The intensive experience of crewing a yacht at sea is accepted as a cost-effective way of providing excellent discipline and leadership training, whilst exposing these young people to an environment which will help them with their own personal development.

The centre has a range of yachts, from the Victoria 34-foot cutters, which are ideal for teaching RYA Qualifications, to the classic Nicholson 55-foot yawls and cutters. The first Nicholson 55 was built for Lloyds of London's Yacht Club in 1970 to replace the first of their *Lutine*'s. This design was so successful that the Services commissioned a special deck moulding and bought a fleet of nine! The most famous of these is *Adventure* which has competed in two Whitbread Round the World Races and has sailed to Australia to join in the bicentennial celebrations. The 'Nic 55's' are regular participants in the Cutty Sark Tall Ships' Races and create a terrific spectacle when sailing in their colour co-ordinated formation of red, white and blue.

**The Yachts**

**Royal Navy** (Blue)
*Adventure*  Cutter rigged, small windows in coach-house, counter stern
*Chaser*  Cutter, retroussé stern
*Dasher*  Cutter, retroussé stern
*Racer*  Cutter, retroussé stern, wooden decks

**Army** (Red)
*Broadsword*  Cutter, retroussé stern, wooden decks
*Kukri*  Cutter, counter stern
*Sabre*  Yawl, counter stern

**Royal Air Force** (White)
*Lord Portal*  Cutter, counter stern
*Lord Trenchard*  Yawl, counter stern

# THE CUTTY SARK TALL SHIPS' RACE WINNERS

**1956 Torbay – Lisbon**
| | | |
|---|---|---|
| Class I | Moyana | UK |
| Class II | Artica II | Italy |

**1958 Brest – La Coruña**
| | | |
|---|---|---|
| Class II | Myth of Malham | UK |

**1958 Brest – Las Palmas**
| | | |
|---|---|---|
| Class I | Sagres | Portugal |
| Class II | L'Etoile | France |
| Class III | Artica II | Italy |

**1960 Oslo – Ostend**
| | | |
|---|---|---|
| Class I | Statsraad Lehmkuhl | Norway |
| Class II | Nordwind | UK |
| Class III | Lutine | UK |

**1960 Cannes – Naples**
| | | |
|---|---|---|
| Class I | Gorch Fock | Germany |
| Class II | Belle Adventure | Monaco |

**1962 Torbay – Rotterdam**
| | | |
|---|---|---|
| Class I | Gorch Fock | Germany |
| Class II | Corsaro II | Italy |
| Class III | Glenan | France |

**1964 Plymouth – Lisbon**
| | | |
|---|---|---|
| Class IIa | Belle Poule | France |
| Class IIb | Tawau | UK |
| Class III | Bloodhound | UK |

**1964 Lisbon – Bermuda**
| | | |
|---|---|---|
| Class I | Christian Radich | Norway |
| Class II | Corsaro II | Italy |
| Class III | Peter Von Danzig | Germany |

**1965 Southsea – Cherbourg**
| | | |
|---|---|---|
| Class B | Urania | Netherlands |
| Class C | Lily Maid | UK |

**1966 Southsea – Cherbourg**
| | | |
|---|---|---|
| Class C | Merlin | UK |

**1966 Falmouth – Skaw**
| | | |
|---|---|---|
| Class A | Sorlandet | Norway |
| Class B1 | Sir Winston Churchill | UK |
| Class B2 | Centurion | UK |
| Class C1 | Zulu | UK |
| Class C2 | Sereine | France |

**1966 Skaw – Den Helder**
| | | |
|---|---|---|
| Class A | Gorch Fock | Germany |
| Class B | Urania | Netherlands |
| Class C | Najade | Netherlands |

**1967 Southsea – Cherbourg**
| | | |
|---|---|---|
| Class B | Duet | UK |
| Class C | Griffin III | UK |

**1968 Gothenberg – Kristiansand**
| | | |
|---|---|---|
| Class A | Gorch Fock | Germany |
| Class B | Gladan | Sweden |

**1968 Harwich – Kristiansand**
| | | |
|---|---|---|
| Class B | Rona | UK |
| Class C1 | Zulu | UK |
| Class C2 | Gawaine | UK |

**1968 Kristiansand – Southsea**
| | | |
|---|---|---|
| Class 1 | Lutine | UK |
| Class 2 | Zulu | UK |

**1968 Portsmouth – Cherbourg**
| | | |
|---|---|---|
| Class B | Malcolm Miller | UK |
| Class C | Griffin III | UK |

**1969 Southsea – Cherbourg**
| | | |
|---|---|---|
| Class 1 | Urania | Netherlands |
| Class 2 | Griffin III | UK |

**1969 Weymouth – St Malo**
| | | |
|---|---|---|
| Class 1 | Halcyon | UK |
| Class 2 | Corabia | Netherlands |

**1970 Plymouth – Tenerife**
| | | |
|---|---|---|
| Class A | Christian Radich | Norway |
| Class B1 | Stella Polare | Italy |
| Class B2 | Najade | Netherlands |

**1970 Plymouth – La Coruña**
| | | |
|---|---|---|
| Class B1 | Hoshi | UK |
| Class B2 | Martlet | UK |

**1970 Weymouth – St Malo**
| | | |
|---|---|---|
| Class B | Urania | Netherlands |

**1970 Southsea – Cherbourg**
| | | |
|---|---|---|
| Class B1 | Asgard | Ireland |
| Class B2 | Rampage | UK |

**1971 Monaco – Porto Cervo**
| | | |
|---|---|---|
| Class B | Belle Poule | France |

**1971 Porto Cervo – Malta**
| | | |
|---|---|---|
| Class B | Belle Poule | France |

**1971 Southsea – Cherbourg**
| | | |
|---|---|---|
| Class B2 | Asgard | Ireland |

**1971 Weymouth – St Malo**
| | | |
|---|---|---|
| Class B1 | Asgard | Ireland |
| Class B2 | Malcolm Miller | UK |

**1972 The Solent – The Skaw**
| | | |
|---|---|---|
| Class A | Dar Pomorza | Poland |
| Class B1 | Malcolm Miller | UK |
| Class B2 | Rona | UK |
| Class B3 | Gryphis | UK |

**1972 Helsinki – Falsterbo**
| | | |
|---|---|---|
| Class A | Christian Radich | Norway |
| Class B1 | Gladan | Sweden |
| Class B2 | Asta | Germany |

**1972 Helgoland – Dover**
| | | |
|---|---|---|
| Class B1 | Cynara | UK |
| Class B2 | Asgard | Ireland |

**1972 Weymouth – St Malo**
| | | |
|---|---|---|
| Class B | Sailing Swiss | Switzerland |

**1972 Southsea – Cherbourg**
| | | |
|---|---|---|
| Class B | Falmouth Packet | UK |

**1973 Weymouth – St Malo**
| | | |
|---|---|---|
| Class B1 | Dodo IV | UK |
| Class B2 | Midsip-Ca | France |

**1973 Firth of Clyde**
| | | |
|---|---|---|
| Class B1 | Hirta | UK |
| Class B2 | Seonamara | |

**1973 Southsea – Cherbourg (1st Race)**
| | | |
|---|---|---|
| Class B1 | Dodo IV | UK |
| Class B2 | Kirah | Switzerland |

**1973 Southsea – Cherbourg (2nd Race)**
| | | |
|---|---|---|
| Class B1 | Sabre | UK |

**1974 Dartmouth – La Coruña**
| | | |
|---|---|---|
| Class B1 | Sabre | UK |
| Class B2 | Marabu | UK |

**1974 La Coruña – Portsmouth**
| | | |
|---|---|---|
| Class B1 | Stella Polaire | Italy |
| Class B2 | Glenan | France |

**1974 St Malo – Portsmouth**
| | | |
|---|---|---|
| Class B1 | Belle Poule | France |
| Class B2 | Vanity | Switzerland |

**1974 Copenhagen – Gdynia**
| | | |
|---|---|---|
| Class A | Tovarishch | USSR |
| Class B1 | America | USA |
| Class B2 | Karin | Germany |

**1975 Ijmuiden – Den Helder**
| | | |
|---|---|---|
| Class B1 | Falken | Sweden |
| Class B2 | Zulu | UK |

**1975 Den Helder – Thames Estuary**
| | | |
|---|---|---|
| Class B1 | Falken | Sweden |
| Class B2 | Barbican | UK |

**1975 Southsea – Cherbourg**
| | | |
|---|---|---|
| Class B1 | Master Builder | UK |
| Class B2 | Uomie | UK |

**1975 Firth of Clyde**
| | | |
|---|---|---|
| Class B1 | Crusade | UK |
| Class B2 | Fiona IV | UK |

**1976 Plymouth – Tenerife**
| | | |
|---|---|---|
| Class A | Tovarishch | USSR |
| Class B1 | Sir Winston Churchill | UK |
| Class B2 | Tenerife | Spain |

**1976 Tenerife – Bermuda**
| | | |
|---|---|---|
| Class A | Tovarishch | USSR |
| Class B1 | Gipsy Moth V | UK |
| Class B2 | Stella Polare | Italy |

**1976 Bermuda – Newport**
| | | |
|---|---|---|
| Class A | Gorch Fock | Germany |
| Class B1 | Ticonderoga | USA |
| Class B2 | Olinka | USA |

**1976 Boston – Plymouth**
| | | |
|---|---|---|
| Class A | Phoenix | Ireland |
| Class B1 | Gipsy Moth V | UK |
| Class BII | Sabre | UK |

**1977 Isle of Wight – Le Havre (Silver Jubilee Race)**
| | | |
|---|---|---|
| Class B1 | Gladan | Sweden |
| Class B2 | Electron of Portsea | UK |

**1978 Gothenburg – Oslo**
| | | |
|---|---|---|
| Class A | Gorch Fock | UK |
| Class B1 | Gratitude | Sweden |
| Class B2 | Sunlight | Norway |

**1978 Great Yarmouth – Oslo**
| | | |
|---|---|---|
| Class B1 | Duet | UK |
| Class B2 | Wyvern | UK |

**1978 Oslo – Harwich**
| | | |
|---|---|---|
| Class A | Kruzenshtern | USSR |
| Class B1 | Sir Winston Churchill | UK |
| Class B2 | Chaser | UK |

**1979 Fowey – Isle of Man**
| | | |
|---|---|---|
| Class B1 | Rona | UK |
| Class B2 | Dasher | UK |

**1979 Round Isle of Man Race**
| | | |
|---|---|---|
| Class B1 | America | USA |
| Class B2 | Carilion of Wight | UK |

**1980 Keil – Karlskrona**
| | | |
|---|---|---|
| Class A | Dar Pomorza | Poland |
| Class B1 | Gratitude | Sweden |
| Class B2 | Falken | Sweden |
| Class B3 | Ritza | USSR |

**1980 Frederikshavn – Amsterdam**
| | | |
|---|---|---|
| Class A | Dar Pomorza | Poland |
| Class B1 | Liv | Norway |
| Class B2 | Peter Von Danzig | Germany |
| Class B3 | Dasher | UK |

**1981 Great Yarmouth – Ostend**
| | | |
|---|---|---|
| Class A | Asgard II | Ireland |
| Class B1 | Malcolm Miller | UK |
| Class B2 | Wishstream | UK |

**1982 Falmouth – Lisbon**
| | | |
|---|---|---|
| Class A | Gorch Fock | Germany |
| Class A2 | Royalist | UK |
| Class B | Falken | Sweden |
| Class C1 | Angele Aline | UK |
| Class C2 | Gryphis | UK |

**1982 Vigo – Southampton**
| | | |
|---|---|---|
| Class A | Dar Mlodziezy | Poland |
| Class A2 | Pogoria | Poland |
| Class B | Gladan | Sweden |
| Class C1 | Duet | UK |
| Class C2 | Vega | USSR |

**1983 Travemunde – Karlskrona**
| | | |
|---|---|---|
| Class B | Gladan | Sweden |
| Class C1 | Colin Archer | Norway |
| Class C2 | Tina V | Germany |
| Class C3 | Iskra (Yacht) | USSR |

**1983 Weymouth – St Malo**
| | | |
|---|---|---|
| Class A2 | Royalist | UK |
| Class B | Malcolm Miller | UK |
| Class C1 | Joana I | Canada |
| Class C2 | Carilion of Wight | UK |

## 1984 St Malo – Bermuda
| | | |
|---|---|---|
| Class A | Dar Mlodziezy | Poland |
| Class B | Zawisza Czarny | Poland |
| Class C1 | Swantje | Germany |
| Class C2 | Dasher | UK |

## 1984 Bermuda – Halifax
| | | |
|---|---|---|
| Class A | Dar Mlodziezy | Poland |
| Class C1 | Carola | Germany |
| Class C2 | Dasher | UK |

## 1984 Sydney (Nova Scotia) – Liverpool
| | | |
|---|---|---|
| Class A | Kruzenshtern | USSR |
| Class C1 | Swantje | Germany |
| Class C2 | Flora | USSR |

## 1984 Frederikshavn – Greenock
| | | |
|---|---|---|
| Class A | Georg Stage | Denmark |
| Class A2 | Royalist | UK |
| Class B | Velsheda | UK |
| Class C1 | Peter Von Danzig | Germany |
| Class C2 | Iskra (Yacht) | USSR |

## 1985 Chatham – Zeebrugge
| | | |
|---|---|---|
| Class A2&B | Sir Winston Churchill | UK |
| Class C1 | Ramrod | UK |
| Class C2 | Liv | Norway |
| Class C3 | Tornado | Poland |

## 1986 Newcastle – Bremerhaven
| | | |
|---|---|---|
| Class A | Kruzenshtern | USSR |
| Class A2 | Royalist | UK |
| Class B | Falken | Sweden |
| Class C1 | Jolie Brise | UK |
| Class C2 | Diana | Germany |
| Class C3 | Monsun | Germany |

## 1986 Larvik – Gothenberg
| | | |
|---|---|---|
| Class A | Kruzenshtern | USSR |
| Class A2 | Royalist | UK |
| Class B | Falken | Sweden |
| Class C1 | Liv | Norway |
| Class C2 | Novik | USSR |
| Class C3 | Tormilind | USSR |

## 1987 Kiel – Norkopping
| | | |
|---|---|---|
| Class A | Kaliakra | Bulgaria |
| Class B | Falken | Sweden |
| Class C1 | Duet | UK |
| Class C2 | Audra | USSR |

## 1987 Stockholm – Ronne
| | | |
|---|---|---|
| Class A | Grossherzogin Elizabeth | Germany |
| Class B | Thor Heyerdhal | Germany |
| Class C1 | Colin Archer | Norway |
| Class C2 | Bieszczady | Poland |

## 1987 Weymouth – Cherbourg
| | | |
|---|---|---|
| Class A2&B | Royalist | UK |
| Class C1 | Grania | UK |
| Class C2 | Tormilind | USSR |

## 1988 Karlskrona – Helsinki
| | | |
|---|---|---|
| Class A | Mir | USSR |
| Class B | Gladan | Sweden |
| Class C1 | Kenilu | Germany |
| Class C2 | Linda | USSR |
| Class C3 | Forward | USSR |

## 1988 Mariehamn – Copenhagen
| | | |
|---|---|---|
| Class A | Sedov | USSR |
| Class B | Gladan | Sweden |
| Class C1 | Kraka | Norway |
| Class C2 | Peter Von Danzig | Germany |
| Class C3 | Iskra (Yacht) | USSR |

## 1989 London – Hamburg
| | | |
|---|---|---|
| Class A | Grossherzogin Elizabeth | Germany |
| Class A2 | Asgard II | Ireland |
| Class B | Malcolm Miller | UK |
| Class C1 | Kenilu | Germany |
| Class C2 | Jomfruen | Sweden |
| Class C3 | Adventure | UK |

## 1989 Hamburg – Travemunde
| | | |
|---|---|---|
| Class A | Mir | USSR |
| Class B | Eendracht | Netherlands |
| Class C1 | Jupiter | USSR |
| Class C2 | Petrel | UK |
| Class C3 | Forward | USSR |

## 1990 Plymouth – La Coruña
| | | |
|---|---|---|
| Class A | Esmeralda | Chile |
| Class A2 | Asgard II | Ireland |
| Class B | Falken | Sweden |
| Class C1 | Morning Star | UK |
| Class C2 | Dark Horse | UK |
| Class C3 | Thiber | Netherlands |

## 1990 Bordeaux – Zeebrugge
| | | |
|---|---|---|
| Class A | Esmeralda | Chile |
| Class A2 | Royalist | UK |
| Class B | Gladan | Sweden |
| Class C1 | Jeune Ariane | France |
| Class C2 | Idlevice of Kip | UK |
| Class C3 | Thiber | Netherlands |

## 1991 Milford Haven – Cork
| | | |
|---|---|---|
| Class A | Eendracht | Netherlands |
| Class A2 | Asgard II | Ireland |
| Class B | Malcolm Miller | UK |
| Class C1 | Cassotis | UK |
| Class C2 | Master Builder | UK |
| Class C3 | Moonduster | Ireland |

## 1991 Cork – Belfast
| | | |
|---|---|---|
| Class A | Sedov | Russia |
| Class A2 | Henryk Rutkowski | Poland |
| Class B | Malcolm Miller | UK |
| Class C1 | Jens Krogh | Denmark |
| Class C2 | Master Builder | UK |
| Class C3 | Insouciance | UK |

**1991 Aberdeen – Delfzijl**

| Class A | Mir | Russia |
|---|---|---|
| Class A2 | Asgard II | Ireland |
| Class B | Malcolm Miller | UK |
| Class C1 | Greater Manchester Challenge | UK |
| Class C2 | Sea Spirit | UK |
| Class C3 | Tormilind | Estonia |

**1992 Karlskrona – Kotka**

| Class A&A2 | Grossherzogin Elizabeth | Germany |
|---|---|---|
| Class B | Den Store Bjorn | Denmark |
| Class C1 | Gratitude | Sweden |
| Class C2 | Novik | Russia |
| Class C3 | Merisissi III | Finland |

**1992 Tallinn – Gdynia**

| Class A&B | Johann Smidt | Germany |
|---|---|---|
| Class C1 | Astrid Finne | Sweden |
| Class C2 | Sparta | Russia |
| Class C3 | Nauticus | Poland |

**1993 Newcastle – Bergen**

| Class A | Statsraad Lehmkhul | Norway |
|---|---|---|
| Class A2 | Henryk Rutkowski | Poland |
| Class B | Gladan | Sweden |
| Class C1 | Frithjof II | Sweden |
| Class C2 | Kranich | UK |
| Class C3 | S:T IV | |

**1993 Larvik – Esbjerg**

| Class A | Statsraad Lehmkhul | Norway |
|---|---|---|
| Class A2 | Henryk Rutkowski | Poland |
| Class B | Johann Smidt | Germany |
| Class C1 | Colin Archer | Norway |
| Class C2 | Peter Von Danzig | Germany |
| Class C3 | British Steel | UK |

# BIBLIOGRAPHY

Sail Training – The Message of the Tall Ships
John Hamilton
Patrick Stephens Ltd

Tall Ships
Maldwin Drummond
Angus & Robertson, Publishers

Sailing Ships of the World
Eric Abranson
Thomas Reed Publications Ltd

The Tall Ships are Sailing
Holly Hollins
David & Charles

Spirit of Sail
John Dyson
The Kingswood Press

Photograph: Cutty Sark Scots Whisky

# INDEX OF TALL SHIPS